iN3

12ap

D0501457

Illustrated Dictionary of
MUSICAL
TERMS

For Peter Corlett
and those other friends for whom
learning is a serious delight

Illustrated Dictionary of
MUSICAL TERMS

Christopher Headington

HARPER & ROW, PUBLISHERS

NEW YORK

Cambridge  London
Hagerstown Mexico City
Philadelphia São Paulo
San Francisco Sydney
1817

Designed and produced by Breslich & Foss,
25 Lloyd Baker Street
London WC1X 9AT

Design: Leslie & Lorraine Gerry
Picture Research: Claire Cockburn

Published in the United States of America
by
Harper & Row, Publishers, Inc,
10 East 53rd Street,
New York, New York 10022

First U.S. Edition
Library of Congress Catalog Card Number:
79–48042

Printed in Great Britain

ISBN 01–18190–01

A cappella
The unaccompanied choral style: literally, 'in church style'.

A piacere
Freely, as regards rhythm, dynamics etc.

A tempo
At the standard, established speed. Used after such markings as **Ritenuto**—i.e., temporary departures from the main tempo of a piece—it indicates a return to that tempo.

Absolute Music
Pure music, neither linked to words nor to other—e.g., pictorial—descriptive ideas. The opposite of programme music.

Absolute Pitch
Also called perfect pitch, this is the precise sense of pitch that allows some musicians to identify or reproduce any note without reference to another already identified. It is a gift and so not easily acquired by training. Among composers, Mozart possessed it, but Wagner and Schumann apparently did not.

Abstract Music
The same as absolute music, though some German writers give this term a pejorative sense implying the dry and academic.

Academy
A scholarly society or teaching institution. Recently the term has also been used in the sense of 'performing society' for chamber orchestras.

Accelerando
Getting faster.

Accent
The stress falling on notes that are naturally louder than others, such as the first beat of a bar. This is dynamic accent. It is less usual, but still correct, to apply the term to two other kinds of emphasis: agogic accent where the note is longer than others, and tonic accent where it is higher. All these may of course be combined.

Acciaccatura
A very short ornamental note leading to another, often immediately above or below.

Accidental
A sign placed before a note to raise or lower its pitch. The sharp raises by a semitone, the flat lowers by a semitone, and the natural restores the note to the norm. Less common are the double sharp and double flat which raise and lower respectively by a whole tone. The sharps or flats (key signature) at the beginning of a piece (and of each line) relate to the key and are not accidentals, which, as the name implies, mark departures from it—except in atonal music, where there is of course no key as such.

Accidentals (left to right): sharp, flat, natural, double sharp, double flat

Accompaniment
The musical support given to a principal part by a subordinate one—e.g., the harpsichord music that underpins the vocal recitatives in Mozart's operas. A solo song may have an accompaniment of this kind, but since Schubert the piano 'accompanist' in a song recital is more of a partner than the word suggests.

Acoustics
The science of sound. It is possible to consider all the physics of sound production under this heading: the way in which sounds are produced by a vibrating

Action

medium—e.g., a string, or the air in a wind instrument—and transmitted through the air to the ear-drum, or by electronic means through a loudspeaker. Besides this, the very nature of musical sound is itself a subject for detailed scientific study. The word acoustics is also often used to refer to the sonic characteristics of halls and other places used for the performance of music. Resonance, or sympathetic vibration, is an important factor, for just as a violin needs its body for the strings to give their best sound, so a hall needs its appropriate shape and choice of wall surfaces for music to sound well. A hall equally suitable for all kinds of vocal and instrumental combinations may be an unrealisable ideal, but all architects today take account of available knowledge in this relatively new subject. It is even possible to adjust the acoustics of a hall after it has been built, as has been done with the Royal Albert Hall and Royal Festival Hall in London.

Action

The movement of parts, usually in a keyboard instrument, though it can also apply to the key mechanism of wood-wind and the pedal mechanism of the harp.

Ad libitum

'At will'—referring to permissible freedom in performing a passage so marked, also the omission (or inclusion) of a passage, instrument or voice.

Adagietto

A speed slightly less slow than *adagio*. Less often, a short *adagio* movement, as in Mahler's 5th Symphony.

The auditorium of the Royal Festival Hall in London, built in 1951. Its acoustics are ideal for orchestral music.

Adagio

A slow tempo, perhaps not so slow as *lento* or *largo*, though not all would agree on this. The Italian word merely means 'at ease' or 'relaxed'.

Added sixth

This chord is in effect a major triad plus the added colouring of the sixth note above its root—e.g., C, E, G, A—and may as such form the final chord of a piece. Examples of such endings include 'Venus' in Holst's *Planets*, Mahler's '*Das Lied von der Erde*' and Stravinsky's Symphony in Three Movements. 'Rather too commercial', Stravinsky later commented wryly—a reference to the very common and facile use of the chord in popular music. The added sixth is often incorrectly 'explained' in reference books as an inversion of a seventh chord on the supertonic, but this is not the way musicians have used it.

Aeolian Mode

See **Modes**.

Aesthetics

The philosophy or psychological study of 'the beautiful'. Like life itself, music may be thought to have its standards, laws and even 'morals'. Thus, just as virtue is preferred to vice and order to chaos, in music we seek for emotional and intellectual pleasure, for some kind of enlightenment—as opposed to the negative qualities of muddle, ugliness or perversity. To be satisfying, however, music need by no means be 'beautiful' in the simple sense of 'pretty', especially if we think of it as a form of psychological drama. This point applies especially to the romantics and moderns; and he who prefers classical poise, elegance and shape may not share another's enthusiasm for a tough work like Berg's *Wozzeck* belonging to a different age and aesthetic climate. The demonstrable logic of Schoenberg's serial music does not necessarily please the aesthetic sense; for as with people, music can be respected but not actually liked—and the opposite. Among the philosophers, Schopenhauer is perhaps the most valuable writer on musical aesthetics. Musicians themselves have so far contributed little to shed light upon this important aspect of their art; and as yet few universities offer teaching in this field, although there are signs that this may be changing.

Affections

The baroque doctrine of the affections was formulated by musical theorists in the early 18th century. 'Affections' here means emotions, of which some twenty were listed, together with a description of the appropriate music to express them—sorrow with slow, sighing melody, for example. It was therefore a theory of music as an emotional language, similar to ideas existing in ancient Greece (Plato wrote on music from this standpoint) and also in oriental music.

Affettuoso

Tenderly. In practice often used for vivid and passionate music while the alternative **Teneramente** is reserved for quieter passages.

Affrettando

Hurrying.

Agitato

Agitated.

Agogic Accent

See **Accent**.

Agréments

A French term for ornaments or grace notes, mainly used of baroque music.

Air

A song. Alternatively, a song-like instrumental piece such as the so-called 'Air on the G String' from Bach's 3rd Orchestral Suite.

Alberti Bass

A left-hand accompanying figure in keyboard (usually piano) music, consisting only of broken-chord figuration and named after a composer (Domenico Alberti, 1710–40) who used it extensively

Alborada

Alberti bass

in his harpsichord sonatas. Even Mozart did not disdain this useful device, employed throughout the Andante of his C major Piano Sonata, K.545.

Alborada

A 'dawn song': the matutinal equivalent of a serenade, but usually an instrumental piece rather than a song. Originally, a Spanish piece for folk oboe and drum. Ravel's *'Alborada del gracioso'* is the best-known piece bearing this title.

Albumblatt

A short instrumental piece, literally a 'page from an album'. Schumann's twenty short piano pieces of Op 124 bear this name.

Aleatory Music

Since about 1945, some composers have produced works in which chance elements are introduced, either during the composition itself (in one piano piece by John Cage, imperfections of the manuscript paper have been allowed to determine the course of the music) or more commonly during performance, where, for example, various sections may be interchanged or combined according to the player's will. Cage (b.1912) has been a pioneer in this field and an influential

An 'aleatory' passage in David Bedford's With 100 Kazoos *in which the players are invited to 'interpret' the peaceful landscape and the sinister winged creatures in turn*

From here until p34 players must try to interpret on their instrument the pictures assigned to them. Each picture interpretation should last about 20 seconds, but the conductor may extend or shorten this depending on how he feels the interpretation is going. Go from one picture to the next without a break

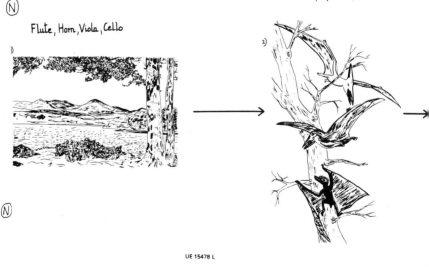

Flute, Horn, Viola, Cello

Clarinet, Trumpet, Vln 2, D-Bass

UE 15478 L

figure. Others who have used aleatory techniques include Boulez, Stockhausen and Xenakis. Computers have been employed also in attempts to generate 'random music', a concept which is in fact quite difficult to realise since the instructions necessarily given tend to create obstacles to the randomness itself.

Aliquot Strings
These are sympathetic strings, not actually struck but serving to reinforce the tone of those that are, fitted by Blüthner among other manufacturers to the high register of pianos.

Alla Breve
The duple time of two minims (half notes) to a bar, indicated commonly by the time signature of $\mathcal{C}$, though writing $\frac{2}{2}$ has the same meaning.

Allargando
Broadening out in speed, perhaps also with increasing fullness of tone.

Allegretto
Fairly lively—i.e., less so than **Allegro**.

Allegro
Lively. The Italian word means 'cheerful', but composers almost invariably use it simply to denote a brisk tempo. (Indeed Poulenc's Clarinet Sonata has an *allegro* first movement marked *tristamente*, sadly). Allegro is the commonest tempo for sonata-form first movements.

Alleluia
The Latin form of a Hebrew exclamation praising God. The alleluia, together with other liturgical words, is sung as part of the Roman Mass except during Lenten and Requiem services.

Allemande
Literally, a German dance. Alternative names include *alman* and *almayne*. As regularly featured in the baroque suites of Bach and others, it has four beats in the bar and a fairly brisk pace.

The allemande, danced in elegant surroundings, evidently permitted amorous badinage. Is the gentleman suggesting some later assignation?

Alt

'High'. A term sometimes used to identify notes in the first octave above the treble stave—e.g., 'G in alt' for the note one octave above treble G.

Alternativo

An old word for the middle section of a piece, later more often called a trio—or more loosely used to suggest the playing of two sections of music in alternation.

Alto

The meaning of 'high' is confusing when used for the low female voice, but is explained by its original use for the *male* alto voice. The alto range, some two octaves with the E above middle C at the centre, is the only one shared by both male and female voices, the male however (sometimes called 'countertenor') being quite distinctive in *timbre*. (The alternative term contralto is only applied to women's voices.)

Alto Clef

The clef used for the viola in orchestral and other scores, having middle C as its middle line. It is also met with in alto-range parts in older music—Palestrina, Bach etc. (See **Clef** for illustration).

Ambrosian Chant

The plainchant melodic style of the Catholic Church named after St Ambrose of Milan (4th century). Though largely superseded by the later re-ordering of church music called Gregorian Chant, it survives today in Ambrose's own cathedral at Milan.

Amoroso

Lovingly, warmly.

Anacrusis

An unstressed note or notes at the start of a phrase; an 'upbeat' effect before a stronger accent.

Analysis

The resolution of a piece of music into its component elements, showing its structure and organic shape. The analytical study of music is perhaps the most important single branch of academic—i.e., musicological—teaching in this subject. At its best, it aims for a fuller understanding of the essence of a musical style and indeed of musical thought itself. The consideration of thematic form (as with Tovey) is the easiest and commonest approach, but other things too—such as melodic and harmonic structure, texture, dynamic shape— invariably repay investigation. Though analysis cannot tell the whole story, it applies to a piece of music as does human physiology to an individual body.

Andante

Literally, a walking pace. As a tempo mark, something less quick than *moderato* but significantly faster than *lento* or *adagio*. *Più andante* should mean faster than *andante*, but occasionally means the opposite where the composer has taken the word just to mean 'slow'.

Andantino

Usually a speed rather less slow than *andante*. But there is some confusion about this (see the *andante* entry above) and the opposite meaning could apply. In Mendelssohn's *Elijah*, incidentally, the same metronome mark is given to two sections, one of which is marked *andante* and the other *andantino*.

Anglican Chant

The traditional chant to English words used in the Anglican (Church of England) service. Unlike plainchant, it is always harmonized, and the main tune is sung by the upper part, trebles or sopranos, sometimes together with the congregation. The tune is repeated with each pair of verses (or in the case of a 'single chant', each verse) in the psalms and canticles.

Animato

Animated, lively.

Answer

In fugue, the second (and in four parts, the fourth also) entry of the main theme.

It differs from the first entry (the subject, in the tonic key) by being at dominant pitch. Thus if the answer (second entry) is a fourth lower than a treble subject, the third entry or 'voice' may be one octave lower. The answer may be a slightly modified version of the subject—for example, to avoid modulation away from the tonic key. It is then called 'tonal', whereas a 'real' answer is note-for-note exact in its relation to the subject.

Antecedent

The first half of a phrase, the second being called the consequent. Alternatively the leading voice in a canon.

Anthem

A religious choral piece to English words: something of an Anglican equivalent to the Catholic (Latin) motet. Commonly there is an organ or other instrumental accompaniment. Sometimes the word just means 'hymn'—as in 'national anthem'. Purcell, Handel and S. S. Wesley are among the important anthem composers.

Antiphon

A short sung passage that precedes and follows a psalm or canticle in the Roman rite, sometimes also standing on its own—e.g., on Palm Sunday.

Antiphonal Style

Alternate singing or playing by different groups.

Appassionato

Passionately, with intense feeling.

Applied Music

Practical music, as opposed to academic or theoretical study: playing or singing instead of book-learning. An American term, mainly.

Appoggiatura

A dissonant ornamental note, leading to another which is consonant and immediately above or below. It falls on the beat and is unhurried in effect.

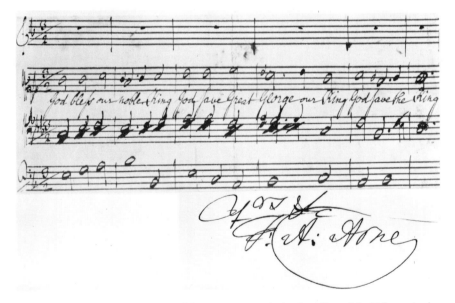

A 1745 version, by Thomas Arne, of the English national anthem (in America, 'My country, 'tis of thee'). The notation is rather casual, the three flats of the E flat major key signature not being written out, and the tune is slightly different from today's.

Appreciation of music

This term implies an element of under-standing going beyond the direct enjoy-ment of music that even a very young child can feel. It has therefore come to be employed for an educational subject, akin to visual or literary critical studies, in which history, analysis and ear train-ing all play a part in enhancing the lis-tener's ability intelligently to hear music. Such a listener is enabled indeed to follow a composer's thought processes with more insight than is possible without training of this kind.

Aquarelle

Literally, a water-colour painting. Applied to music—e.g., in Fenby's string orches-tral arrangements of two Delius pieces—it suggests a delicate miniature.

Arabesque

An ornamental figure or flourish, the musical equivalent of the architectural feature so named. The arabesques for piano by Schumann and Debussy have a lilting and graceful character.

Arco

Bow. As a performing direction in string music, it tells the player to resume bowing after a plucked (*pizzicato*) passage.

Aria

Air—i.e., song. Commonly the term is reserved for opera and oratorio, recital songs being simply called songs. The aria form is normally ternary, with middle section and return, whereas recital songs are more often in strophic or verse form. In opera, the aria is a solo given to a main character; like a soliloquy in a play, it embodies an emotional state and pro-vides a point of rest in the narrative action.

Arietta

A short aria, perhaps without the con-trasting middle section of the full-length aria. In French opera, the term has been more loosely used and may imply some element of lightness or brilliance.

Arioso

A style of singing somewhere between the structured melodic phrases of aria and the highly informal recitative. Beethoven borrows the term for an instrumental passage of this melodic kind in his Piano Sonata Op. 110. Though an adjective in Italian, *arioso* is used as a noun to describe a section of music in this style.

Arpeggio

A broken chord—i.e., the notes of a chord played in sequence rather than simultaneously.

Arrangement

A reworking of an original piece of music. It may be for another instrument or instrumental combination, and even vocal pieces have been arranged for piano or orchestra. Or it may be a simplified version for the same instrument. More loosely, it can involve some elaboration and extension of the original notes—but this is nowadays more properly called a transcription, the word we apply to Liszt's versions for piano of operatic music by Verdi and Wagner. Some writ-ers use these two terms indiscriminately however, and in America they can have the opposite meanings to those given here—i.e., the arrangement being the freer treatment.

Ars Antiqua

The 'ancient art' of early polyphonic composers around 1160–1300, begin-ning with Léonin and Pérotin who were consecutive choirmasters at Notre Dame in Paris. Their work, based on plain-chant, is in from two to four vocal parts. The Latin motet is an important product of this period. Triple rhythms were also a feature of 13th-century style.

Ars nova

This term, used by 1325, denotes the fresh style in both sacred and secular music which followed that of the more formal *ars antiqua*. Duple rhythm and syncopation, as well as generally greater melodic freedom, are among features of the *ars nova*. Guillaume de Machaut

(1300–77) is among the most important musicians, composing the first complete Mass setting by a single writer. The Italian Landini (1325–97), a master of expressive harmony, and the Englishman Dunstable (1380–1453) are other prominent figures in a period of experiment which opened up the way to the wide-ranging Josquin des Prés (1450–1521) and the humanistic style of the Renaissance.

Arsin et thesin

Originally used of weak and strong accents—and still so used by some French and German theorists—this rather uncommon Greek term is now mainly employed in reference to a canon or other contrapuntal piece where either (a) the tune in the first voice is inverted in the second, or (b) the pattern of strong and weak beats is reversed in the second voice.

Articulation

Musical shaping and phrasing: the clear and conscious delivery of the notes that music needs if it is not to sound mechanical or lifeless. This is most obviously necessary for a singer, who must use accent, breathing, legato/staccato contrast, vocal colour and so on to 'put over' his text both verbally and musically, but it is not less essential for a solo instrumentalist. One of the chief functions of a conductor, too, is the imparting of an overall articulation to orchestral phrasing, and similarly the leader of a string quartet will guide the four players so that they phrase alike.

Assai

Literally, 'very'—thus *allegro assai* properly means a very lively tempo. But it seems that some composers, probably including Beethoven, used this word like the French *assez*, meaning 'fairly'. Thus the *allegro assai* of Beethoven's 'Appassionata' Sonata for piano is less rather than more *allegro* in speed.

Atonality

The absence of tonality, of the use of a key system; the musical style characterized by such a method. Music that fully embraces atonal methods belongs exclusively to the 20th century and its prophet was the Viennese composer Arnold Schoenberg (1874–1951) with such works as *Pierrot Lunaire* (1912). Following upon the freely non-tonal writing of *Pierrot* or the Piano Pieces, Op 11, Schoenberg's later serial or twelve-note technique was systematically atonal and this new compositional method proved influential even though its wide adoption by composers (and acceptance by audiences) seems impossible.

Attacca

Go straight on—i.e., continue without a clear pause from one movement or section to the next.

Attack

Decisiveness, especially in beginning a phrase or single note. It may imply a vigorous *forte*, but in orchestral terms can equally mean a well-coordinated *pianissimo* entry. The French call an orchestral leader (concertmaster) the *chef d'attaque*.

Aubade

A dawn song: the morning equivalent of a serenade. Bizet, Rimsky-Korsakov and Poulenc have employed the term. Wagner's *Siegfried Idyll* (1870), written to awaken his wife as a surprise present on her birthday morning, is the best-known of all aubades, even though not so-called.

Augmentation

The lengthening of note-values, usually by doubling them. Used in a fugue, normally towards the end, the device is applied to the subject (main theme) and lends breadth and dignity.

Augmented Sixth

A triad chromatically altered so that its outer notes form an augmented interval—for example, in C major the chord A, C, F (its outer notes forming a minor 6th) can become A flat, C, F sharp. Commonly the chord resolves outwards on to the dominant (G, B, D, G) and may

Autograph

Augmented Sixths (left to right): Italian Sixth, French Sixth, German Sixth

then be followed by the tonic C, E, G in a perfect cadence.

Autograph

A manuscript copy of a piece of music in the composer's own hand.

Auxiliary Note

A non-harmonic—i.e., dissonant—ornamental melody note that is approached from the note immediately below or above and then returns to the note originally sounded.

Ayre

Old English spelling for 'air'. In theory the same as *aria*; but in practice an ayre is an English song, such as those with lute by Dowland (1563–1626) and others of his time.

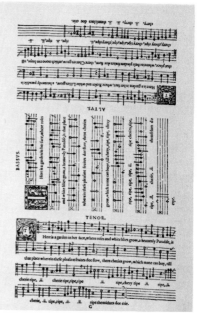

The layout of this ayre by Robert Jones permitted performance by four singers seated around a table.

B

Badinerie

A light-hearted dance movement, with two beats in a bar, mainly in 18th-century music. An example is the final movement of Bach's Suite in B minor for flute and strings.

Bagatelle

Literally, a trifling or slight piece of music. But those for piano by Beethoven are more serious in tone than the name implies and only slight in their duration. One might think that Beethoven's original German word *Kleinigkeiten* meant simply miniatures and had been mis-translated, but it is the exact equivalent of the French word *bagatelle*.

Ballad

Though this word, like 'ballet', is related to the Italian *ballare* (to dance), and did at one time imply a 'song for dancing', it now has nothing at all to do with the dance. It is used for poems and songs alike, the latter usually fairly simple, nar-rative and appearing in England from the 15th century. Ballads were sometimes printed just as poems with some such instruction as 'to be sung to the tune of "Greensleeves"' and then sold in the streets. In Victorian England the word was used for songs of a drawing-room kind like Sullivan's 'The Lost Chord'.

Ballade

No more a dance than the ballad (see above), nor a song, but instead a longish instrumental piece, commonly for piano solo. Chopin's four ballades are pro-totypes, akin to the poetic ballades of his compatriot Mickiewicz, their music being narrative and dramatic in feeling though without any specific literary programme. Later ballades include those

by Brahms, Liszt, Grieg, Debussy, and one for piano and orchestra by Fauré.

Ballad Opera

A theatrical piece in which songs and spoken dialogue alternate, popular in style and characteristic of the English stage in the early 18th century. The most celebrated of all is John Gay's *The Beg-gar's Opera*, produced in London in 1728. As the title suggests, it was something of a popular answer to the serious operatic style as exemplified by Handel (then busy writing operas for London audi-ences) and the music by Pepusch was arranged from popular tunes rather than specially composed. Later ballad operas include those by Arne (*Love in a Village*, 1726) and Vaughan Williams (*Hugh the Drover*, 1924). Kurt Weill's *The Three-penny Opera* of 1928 is a modern German reworking of *The Beggar's Opera* in jazz style; Britten also made a new version in 1948.

Harmony, with back turned, seems to repudiate the rough-and-ready goings-on in this lampoon of The Beggar's Opera. *Presumably the elegantly dressed 'animals' on the stage are less than refined vocalists*

Ballata

An Italian song form of the period around 1400, indeed perhaps the most important contribution of Italy to the *ars nova* period that preceded the renaissance. A ballata could be for one or more voices. Each verse had a pattern of musical phrases corresponding to its lines, viz. A, B, B, A, A.

Ballet

The most sophisticated form of dancing, performed with orchestra in a theatre before an audience, just as an opera is. Like opera, a ballet tells a story although without a spoken or sung text, this being achieved by dance movements involving the whole body and also by the character of the music itself. As the French name suggests, the origin of ballet is to be found in France, particularly that of Louis XIV and his court composer Lully. The *ballet de cour*, in which the King himself liked to dance, was a stately affair, but the *comédie-ballet* created by Lully and Molière together was more of a public spectacle. It was another Frenchman, Noverre (1727–1810), who created the real dramatic, story-telling ballet, the *ballet d'action*, establishing the full-length ballet performance and collaborating with Gluck and Mozart, whose *Les petits riens* dates from 1778. Noverre also wrote an influential treatise on his art.

Mozart's *Les petits riens* was produced in Vienna as well as Paris, and the ballet spread widely from France in the 18th and 19th centuries. It was in Russia that the most musically important of 19th-century ballets were produced, these being those with choreography by the Marseillais Marius Petipa (1822–1910) and music by Tchaikovsky—*Swan Lake* (1877), *The Sleeping Beauty* (1890) and *The Nutcracker* (1892). After 1900, it was Diaghilev who created the celebrated *Ballets russes* who came to take Paris by storm in 1909. Stravinsky was Diaghilev's most important collaborator in the years immediately prior to World War I with *The Firebird*, *Petrushka* and *The Rite of Spring*.

Ballet Rambert perform Glen Tetley's modern ballet, Pierrot Lunaire, *with music by Schoenberg.*

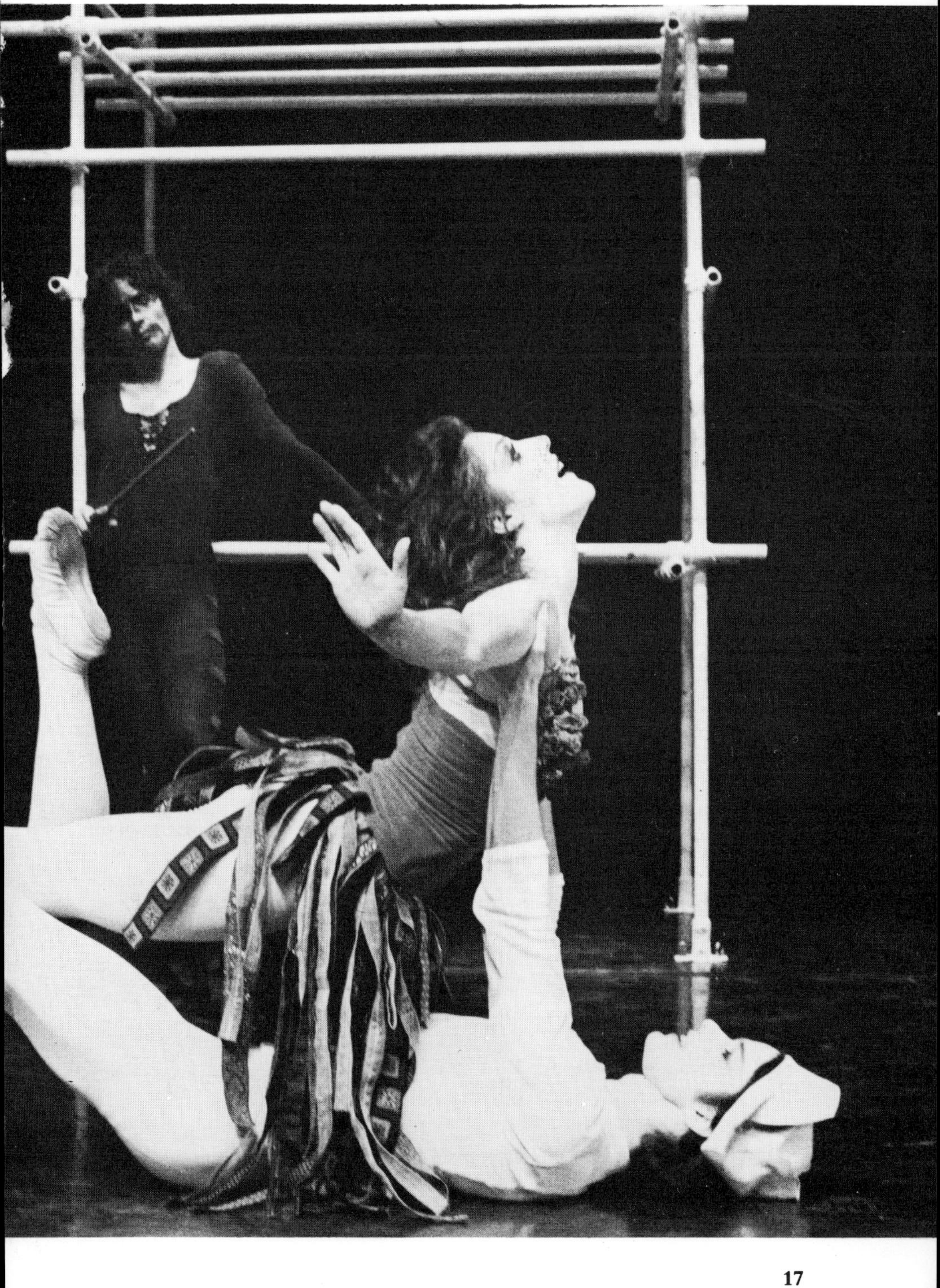

(Top) A Florentine equestrian and military ballet celebrating the arrival of the Prince of Urbino
(Above) Swan Lake: the 1895 production of Tchaikovsky's famous ballet in St Petersburg

The ballet is now an established part of theatrical life in most capital cities in the more affluent parts of the world. Among 20th-century composers who have written ballet music we may mention Ravel, Debussy, Satie and Poulenc in France and, among the Russians, Stravinsky, Prokofiev and Shostakovich. Other names include Bartók, Vaughan Williams, Britten, Copland and Bernstein. Apart from music specially composed for ballet, many existing scores have been used for this purpose—for example, one of the most celebrated of all ballets, *Les Sylphides*, is a marriage of Fokine's choreography with an orchestral version of various piano pieces by Chopin. A whole range of the musical repertory from Bach to Boulez has with varying success thus been put to an artistic purpose for which it was not designed.

It is worth briefly adding that ballet sections are an essential part of musical shows like Bernstein's *West Side Story* (1957) and common also in opera, where we find such numbers as the *Sailors' Dance* in Purcell's *Dido and Aeneas* (1689), the *Polovtsian Dances* of Borodin's *Prince*

Igor (1887) and the *Dance around the Golden Calf* in Schoenberg's *Moses und Aaron* (1954). There are dance sections of importance in Britten's opera *Death in Venice* (1973), where indeed one of the principal characters is not a singer but a dancer.

Band

A large or fairly large instrumental group, nowadays predominantly of wind instruments—e.g., a brass or military band. The brass band is normally made up exclusively of brass instruments plus percussion, and includes cornets and saxhorns as well as trombones. The military band, besides these instruments, has a full complement of woodwind also, the numerous clarinets (ten or more) playing much the same melodic role as the violins in a symphony orchestra. In a jazz band we find, in various combinations and numbers, the trumpet, trombone, clarinet, saxophone, string bass, piano and drums. Any dance orchestra is likely to call itself a 'band'—a balalaika band etc.

Bar

A measure of music, marked by the vertical bar lines drawn in the stave.

Bar Form

A German song form of medieval and renaissance times. The overall shape may be represented as A, A, B—called in German the two *Stollen* (strophes) and the *Abgesang* (after-song). Wagner includes a description of the form in Act III of *Die Meistersinger*. It has indeed been argued that the large-scale use of bar form is the main structural principle in *Meistersinger* as a whole and perhaps elsewhere in Wagner's operas.

Barcarolle

Literally, a boat song of the Venetian gondoliers. In practice, a vocal or instrumental piece in a lapping, gentle rhythm, 6/8 or 12/8. Among songs,

John Philip Sousa (front row, centre) and his band in Hamburg, 30 May 1900

Hans Breuer

SOUSA AND HIS BAND
Hamburg. Germany May 30. 1900.

Hamburg Pferdemarkt No. 27.

Schubert's '*Auf dem Wasser zu singen*' and Offenbach's '*Barcarolle*' in *The Tales of Hoffmann* may be cited, while Chopin's Op 60 for piano is undoubtedly the most celebrated of instrumental barcarolles.

Bard

A poet–singer of the medieval and earlier periods, working in an oral tradition that goes back to the ancient Greeks (Orpheus, Homer) and doubtless still further. The bardic style and tradition survives today in the Welsh *eisteddfod* or bardic gathering. The traditional instrument of the Welsh bards is the *crwth*, a relative as its name suggests of the ancient Greek *kithara*.

Baritone

The medium–range male voice, below tenor and above bass. The range is about one and a half octaves upwards from the bottom G of the bass stave. The instrument called the baritone is one of the saxhorn family and is to be found in brass bands.

Baroque Music

Roughly, music belonging to that period between 1600 and 1750 which includes such composers as Monteverdi, Purcell, Lully, Rameau, Bach and Handel. During this time the major and minor key system wholly replaced the old modes of renaissance music, and larger instrumental forms such as the suite, fugue and concerto grosso came into being. The birth of opera and oratorio, which took place in Italy, coincides with the beginning of the baroque period. The word baroque itself comes from architecture and has no musical significance, serving merely to identify this important part of musical history.

(Left) The most famous among the bards of antiquity: Orpheus with his lyre, in a Sicilian mosaic of the 2nd century

(Above) The solid splendours of a baroque orchestra, in the gallery of the Jesuit Hall in Munich

In baroque music, strong formal organization is often accompanied by highly dramatic expressive technique; it was during this time that such effects as *crescendo* and *diminuendo* were first fully exploited, for example in the operatic orchestra. The orchestra itself also developed rapidly, its varying textures and instrumental colours greatly enriching the expressive resources of music. Monteverdi was one of the first masters in this sphere. Contrasts, he declared, were what moved his listeners, and there is a parallel here with the dramatic light-and-shade *chiaroscuro* technique of painting.

Barré

In guitar and lute playing, a technique of holding the forefinger across several (or all) of the strings and so shortening their effective length.

Bass

The low male voice. Its choral compass is about one and a half octaves above low F (the F just below the bass stave) though soloists frequently go both lower and higher, and Russian basses in particular are famous for fine clear notes down to low C. As an adjective, 'bass' refers to voices or low-pitched instruments, though the bass flute hardly reaches downwards into the bass clef and is more correctly called an alto. A 'bass part' or 'bass line' is the lowest in a texture.

Basse Danse

A western European dance form of the 15th and 16th centuries. Presumably the feet were kept close to the ground and moved in a gliding way—which they were not, for example, in the *pied en l'air* step of more vigorous dancing. Moderate speed and duple time are characteristic. There is an example in Warlock's 'Capriol' Suite, taken from a collection dated 1589.

The basse danse *with its gliding step*

Baton

The conductor's stick, the modern-style light stick dating only from the 19th century. Not all conductors use a baton: choral conductors in particular sometimes feel they can mould the music more expressively with the hands alone.

Beat

The regular pulse of music. The downbeat is strong, the upbeat weak. In acoustics, a beat is an audible regular pulse resulting from coinciding moments in two close but different frequencies. As the two frequencies converge towards the unison, the speed of these decreases and finally the beats stop altogether, so that this phenomenon is thus useful in tuning, say unison strings. The undulating 'beats' effect is used in two organ stops, the *unda maris* and *voix céleste*.

Bebop

See **Bop**.

Bebung

A vibrating effect possible only on the clavichord, where after a note has been played the sound may still be affected by changing the finger pressure on the depressed key. Some repeated-note passages in Beethoven's piano music are sometimes thought to aim at some kind of imitation of this technique.

Bel canto

Literally, 'beautiful song'. A lyrical and tonally beautiful singing style that was especially the province of Italian singers in the 18th century, for example in the Neapolitan operas of Alessandro Scarlatti (1660–1725).

Bell

The bell-shaped opening of a wind instrument such as the horn.

Ben

Well—e.g., *ben marcato*, well marked.

Berceuse

A cradle song or lullaby, usually instrumental however and in a gentle duple time. Perhaps the best known is the piano Berceuse of Chopin (1844).

Bergamasque
Deriving its name from the Bergamo district of Northern Italy, this was originally a popular, dance-like piece. Shakespeare's rustics in *A Midsummer Night's Dream* offer to dance a 'bergomask'. Debussy's *Suite bergamasque* for piano, which includes the famous '*Clair de lune*', has little Italian about it and evidently is intended only to evoke a pastoral scene.

Bicinium
A 16th-century composition in two polyphonic parts, vocal or instrumental.

Binary Form
Two-section form. Many of Bach's shorter movements, such as the keyboard inventions, use this form. The first part modulates to the dominant or relative major, while the second (not essentially different in material) returns to the tonic key.

Bitonality
The use of two keys simultaneously. The famous combination of C major and F sharp major arpeggios in Stravinsky's *Petrushka* (1911) (anticipated in fact by Ravel ten years earlier in *Jeux d'eau*) is really not bitonal in the fullest sense, which implies a real use together of two keys with their whole range of associated harmonies and melodic lines. For this we find an example in Charles Ives, whose organ variations upon the tune 'America' (1891) has an uncompromising F major—A flat major combination. In the 20th century, several composers have employed bitonality, but only with Milhaud do we feel that the technique is essential and significant. It seems that, in all save brief and characteristic passages, the effect is confusing and unsatisfying to the ear. Nevertheless the brief bitonal flashes in such a piece as Copland's orchestral *El Salon México* are brilliantly witty and successful, not least because of the clarity of rhythms and textures.

Block Chords
Alternatively called parallel chords. A 20th-century use of chords foreign to traditional diatonic—i.e., major-minor— harmonic methods. A chord—a major or minor triad, or even a dissonant chord— is used to decorate each note of a melody, without however destroying the sense of key. Debussy is perhaps the composer who made block-chord writing especially a feature of his style.

Blues
An American jazz idiom, its vocal style and intensity of mood deriving from the black spiritual. Sometimes a lamenting love song—e.g., 'Empty Bed Blues', 'St Louis Blues'. As a form, the blues has 12-bar phrases, 'blue' flattened 3rd and 7th degrees of the scale giving a tense minor-mode feeling in the melody above accompanying major chords which pulsate steadily, one each beat. The vocal style is sustained and the speed slow. However, a faster Texas style of blues exists to contrast with the slower blues of New Orleans and St Louis.

John Henry Fortescue ('Guitar Shorty') sings the blues in 1972 in North Carolina.

Boehm System

Metal keywork for the flute invented around 1830 by Theobald Boehm (1793–1881), allowing the holes to be cut in their best acoustical places while remaining easily operable by the hand. The Boehm instrument is generally easier to play than its predecessor, and is now universally adopted for flutes. Variants have also been used on oboes and clarinets, more rarely on bassoons.

Bolero

A Spanish dance form in triple time and played at moderate speed, characteristically with castanets in the accompaniment. Ravel's orchestral 'Bolero' (1928) is a famous example. A Cuban dance of the same name has a different, duple rhythm.

Boogie-Woogie

Piano jazz style first heard in 1920s Chicago. A short repeated left-hand figure in the bass—i.e. an *ostinato*—provides an accompaniment to free and florid right-hand figuration. The speed is rapid and the mood highly energetic.

Bop

This jazz style (also called bebop) developed with performers such as Charlie Parker and Dizzy Gillespie and is predominantly an instrumental technique. Rhythmically it is quite unlike older jazz in being very free as regards the regular beat and in its use of dissonant harmony. Bop evolved into the cooler improvisatory style of 1950s jazz—Kenton, Monk, Brubeck, Davis. The name probably derives from the nonsense 'patter' syllables that were occasionally sung. Bop is characteristically very fast and 'flickering' in articulation.

Bouche fermée

Literally, 'with mouth closed'—an instruction to singers, usually in a choral texture, to hum. An example occurs in Debussy's orchestral 'Sirènes'. An alternative, easier for the performer, is to sing with the mouth open but the teeth closed.

Bouffons

A vigorous 16th-century dance, originally a sword dance by men in stage armour of gilded cardboard. Alternatively called *matassins* or *mattachins*, this word deriving from Arabic.

Bourdon

A drone or pedal point—i.e., a long note sustained beneath changing harmonies. Also the largest bell in a set, and a low-pitched organ stop. Not the same as **Burden**.

Bourrée

Lively French dance, often found in baroque instrumental suites such as Bach's. Characteristically, two minims (half notes) to the bar and beginning on the crotchet (quarter note) before the bar line.

Bowing

The art of using the bow of a stringed instrument. There are various bowing techniques. Among these are *legato*, involving a flexible wrist at the change of direction from down-bow to up-bow, and *staccato*, with the bow bouncing on the string or momentarily stopped in its movement between the notes.

Branle

15th-century French country dance, in its duple versions similar to the **Gavotte** though more rustic. The word *branler* means 'to sway'. The triple-time *branle gay* and the duple *branle double* are both employed by Stravinsky in his ballet *Agon* (1957). (He uses the alternative older spelling *bransle*.) Shakespeare refers to this dance as a 'brawl' in *Love's Labour's Lost*, when the page Moth asks Armado, 'will you win your love with a French brawl?'.

(Right) Bowing action, illustrated in the Violinschule *of Ferdinand David (1810–73), the first interpreter of Mendelssohn's Violin Concerto*

Brass Band
See **Band**.

Bravura
Brilliant execution or display.

Break
An extemporized solo in jazz. Also the change from treble to adult male voice.

Breve
Note equivalent to four minims (half notes). Written ‖𝗈‖ . Comparatively rare in modern music, save as a conventional notation for a long and unmeasured sustained note—e.g., against a short cadenza.

Bridge
The slim wooden support which holds the strings of an instrument away from the body and transmits their vibrations to the instrument as a whole.

Fig.III.

Fig.I.

Fig.IV.

Fig.II.

Fig.V.

Fig.VII.

Fig.VI.

Bridge Passage

A passage of music linking two thematic sections, by implication or perhaps even definition subordinate in musical content to what precedes and follows. Frequently a bridge passage effects a modulation between first and second subjects in the exposition of a sonata-form movement, and disappears or changes in the recapitulation.

Brillante

Brilliant in style. A performing direction.

Brio

Vigour, spirit.

Broken Chord

The notes of a chord played individually rather than simultaneously. If there is a difference between the near-synonymous terms of broken chord and arpeggio it is that the notes of the former need not be in order of pitch.

Buffo

Light, comic: a *basso buffo* is a singer for comic roles in Italian opera. Leporello in Mozart's *Don Giovanni*, and Falstaff in Verdi's Shakespearian opera of that name, are *buffo* roles, though both these characters have more to them than simple humour. The Italian word *buffo* suggests a puff of air, in other words extreme lightness of touch.

Burden

A recurring line or musical phrase, a refrain.

Burlesque

A piece of playful character, alternatively called *burla*—e.g., Strauss's *Burleske* for piano and orchestra. A burlesque show is an English and especially American theatrical entertainment that may derive from ballad opera, topical and distinctly 'lowbrow', including in modern times striptease spectacles.

Byzantine Chant

The plainchant style of the Christian Church in the Eastern Roman Empire (330–1453), whose capital, now Istanbul in Turkey, was formerly called Byzantium. The texts were in Greek but the musical style was akin to that of the Latin Gregorian chant—unaccompanied, diatonic and rhythmically free.

cadenza to link a preceding movement to the finale. Up to Beethoven's time, a cadenza was improvised, but nowadays it is always written out. The rare accompanied cadenza features in the finale of Elgar's Violin Concerto.

Cambiata
A melodic pattern variously defined, and also sometimes called 'changing notes'. It usually involves a leap of a third.

Cambiata

Cabaletta
A short operatic aria with repeated rhythmic figures, or (in Verdi) a final section in this style.

Caccia
A two-part canon with added bass line, from 14th-century Italy. The text is topical and vivid—street scenes, hunting etc. The word itself means 'chase' or hunt and can also be thought to apply to the 'pursuit' of the one voice by the other. The French had a *chace*, usually a canon in three parts.

Camera
A chamber or room. Hence *musica da camera* is chamber music, *orchestra da camera* a chamber orchestra. The baroque *sonata de camera* is really a suite consisting of an introduction and three or four

Cadence
A two-chord progression that closes a musical sentence, either fully or partially.

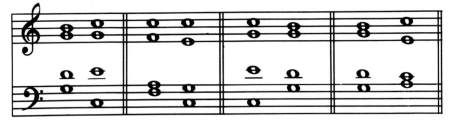

Cadences (left to right): Perfect, Plagal, Imperfect, Interrupted (all in C major)

Cadenza
A display section for solo voice or instrument, unaccompanied, occurring towards the end of an aria or concerto movement. The traditional place for a concerto cadenza is after the recapitulation in the first movement, but Beethoven places a cadenza at the start of his Fifth Piano Concerto and Mendelssohn in his Violin Concerto has a cadenza at the end of the development section of the first movement. In their violin concertos Britten and Shostakovich (No 1) use a

dances, characteristically written for two violins with accompaniment of harpsichord and string bass.

Can-Can
A vigorous and frivolous Parisian dance of the 19th century, in duple rhythm and fast. The most famous example is in Offenbach's *Orpheus in the Underworld* (1847). (See illustration overleaf)

Cancel
Same as 'natural'—as opposed to sharp, flat, etc. See **Accidental** for illustration.

Cancrizans

(Above) The can-can as danced at the
Moulin Rouge in Paris, 1889

Cancrizans

Retrograde—i.e., backwards—motion,
in which the notes of a previously heard
melody are replayed or re-sung in reverse
order. The device is rare, but occurs, for
example, in the finale of Beethoven's
'Hammerklavier' Piano Sonata.

Canon

Literally, rule or law—a strict musical
form which has the individual voices or
instrumental parts taking up a tune in
turn in exact imitation and following
each other at an interval in time such as
one bar. As regards pitch, the voices may
be at the interval of the octave, fifth or
any other the composer chooses. Bach's
'Goldberg' Variations for harpsichord
contain ingenious canons at various
intervals. The same composer's *Musical
Offering* has further canonic devices such
as a combination of augmentation and
inversion—doubling the note values of
the following part and also turning it
upside down.

Cantabile
In a singing style. Applied to instrumental music (perhaps most commonly in piano music) as a performing direction that implies some emphasis upon the melodic line and an expressive delivery (in dynamics, tone, rhythmic flexibility) of its phrases.

Cantata
A vocal work. The term was used in baroque times, by Bach for example, usually to mean an extended choral piece based on the melody and verses structure of a church chorale. Bach also wrote secular cantatas—his 'Coffee' Cantata is a miniature opera in all but name—while Handel's Italian dramatic cantatas are also operatic in style. A more modern example such as Debussy's *L'enfant prodigue* (1884) is narrative in a way that relates to oratorio, as is also Britten's *St Nicolas* (1948).

Cante Flamenco
Andalusian melodic song style, though also used for the dance. An intense and sometimes melancholy mood is characteristic, as is the improvisatory freedom. The accompaniment is provided by the guitar, hence the traditional use of the E minor tonality which so suits that instrument.

Cante Hondo
Literally, 'deep song': possibly the main precursor of the *flamenco* style. Originally a tragic-toned prisoners' song.

Canticle
A Christian hymn, such as the Magnificat. Alternatively an extended song to a religious text (but not intended for use in a church service) such as the five canticles composed by Britten, one of which (No 2) tells the story of Abraham and Isaac.

Cantilena
Vocal melodic style of lyrical, perhaps intimate character; also a short song in this style. Occasionally the term is applied to instrumental music of a similar nature.

Cantor
The director of music or choirmaster in a German Protestant church. Alternatively the precentor—i.e., leading singer—in a Jewish synagogue.

Cantus firmus
A melody used, from the 13th century onwards, to provide one vocal or instrumental part for a polyphonic composition. Such a melody is pre-existent—for example a plainchant tune or (with Bach) a German chorale—while the added parts are specially composed.

(Left) Six voices here sing a canonic tune in C major, entering at four-bar intervals. The second phrase (reading from the top clockwise) is in the bass clef, the ground bass that may accompany the tune throughout

Canzona

The word has been variously used, but most often means a short composition for instrumental ensemble. Also a vocal composition, ensemble or solo, in the former case akin to the madrigal and perhaps operatic.

Canzonet

Short vocal piece, ensemble or solo. Haydn composed twelve 'canzonettas' to English words for voice and piano, published in 1794–5.

Canzonet

Short vocal piece, ensemble or solo. Haydn composed twelve 'canzonettas' to English words for voice and piano, published in 1794–5.

Cappella

Literally, 'chapel'. The term refers to music that is unaccompanied—i.e., 'in the church style' of earlier times. The word can also mean a choir or other ensemble; hence the German term *Kapellmeister* for both 'choirmaster' and 'orchestral director'.

Capriccio

Light, fanciful, solo instrumental piece. The term is most frequently applied to keyboard music, though Rimsky-Korsakov's *Capriccio espagnol* for orchestra and Tchaikovsky's *Capriccio italien* (also orchestral) are exceptions. The word 'caprice' is more broadly used (Paganini's for unaccompanied violin are famous).

Carmen

A Latin word for a song or poem: the word is occasionally used in vocal writing of the early renaissance and even for instrumental music of similar character.

Carol

A Christmas song of appropriately joyful character. The older French *carole* was a round dance probably associated with pagan dance-songs marking the winter solstice. Scholars also remember the medieval carol as a musical form with

(Above) A French round dance or carole: *the picture is from the 13th-century poem* 'Le Roman de la Rose'.

verses and refrains, not always linked with Christmas.

Cassation

An 18th-century ensemble instrumental piece intended for outdoor performance. There are examples by both Haydn and Mozart for mixed wind and strings. Much the same as a divertimento in style—i.e., music for entertainment.

Castrato

Male adult singer of the late renaissance and baroque periods whose unbroken boy's voice has been preserved by surgical operation. The most famous *castrati* of the operatic stage in Handel's time (around 1700–50) were greatly admired for their skill in using a voice combining the soprano range with a man's powerful chest and lungs.

(Right) The celebrated castrato *singer Farinelli (1705–82) in an operatic role*

Catch

A round—i.e., a canon in which the voices keep returning to their starting point. A particularly English musical style, popular after the Restoration (1660) and often with bawdy, good-humoured words.

Cavatina

Short song in an opera, similar to an arietta. The term is occasionally employed for instrumental music in this style. Beethoven's String Quartet Op 130 has a slow movement marked 'cavatina'.

Cembalo

Harpsichord.

Cent

One hundredth part of a semitone. The measure is useful in acoustics though hardly so in practical music-making.

Chaconne

A variation-form instrumental piece in which the 'theme' is essentially a sequence of harmonies. Purcell's G minor Chacony for strings and the finale of Brahms's Fourth Symphony are examples.

(Above) The (mainly) wind ensemble of Prince Oettingen-Wallerstein, in 1791. The ten players are about the maximum number for chamber music.

Chamber Music

Instrumental ensemble music for up to ten or so players. The main difference between chamber and orchestral music is that in chamber music there is only one player to each part. Perhaps less obviously, chamber music is, as the name implies, intended for a room rather than a public hall and thus primarily for the enjoyment of the performers rather than that of an audience; a more intimate style is therefore characteristic. In chamber music, the string quartet corresponds in importance with the orchestral symphony.

(Left) The chaconne, here called cicona, *was originally a Mexican or Spanish dance. Here a gipsy girl with castanets dances it with a 'black magician'.*

Chant

Literally, a song; but in practice the word normally refers to church singing of the psalms and canticles. Roman Catholic plainchant is sung in unison, often unaccompanied and rhythmically free. The Anglican chant of English parish churches is harmonized and usually accompanied by the organ. In both cases the chant melody is short and in two phrases corresponding to the two halves of a verse.

Characteristic Piece

A very general 19th-century term for a short instrumental piece having a definite mood, such as a *moment musical*, bagatelle or 'song without words'. Debussy's piano preludes would also fall into this category.

Charleston

Lively dance of the 1920s, akin to the foxtrot and named after the South Carolina city. In 4/4 time, the emphasis on the first and fourth quavers (8th notes) producing strong syncopation.

Chance Music

Another name for **Aleatory Music**.

Changing Note

Another name for **Cambiata**. Also a melodic pattern of the following type:

Chanson

A song. Mainly used in medieval and renaissance times for solo and polyphonic vocal compositions, the latter sometimes French madrigals. The modern French word for a recital song— the equivalent of the German *Lied*—is however *mélodie*.

The 'naughty twenties' captured as Bee Jackson dances the Charleston

33

Chest Voice
The lower register of a voice, male or female.

Chiesa
Literally, church. The baroque *sonata da chiesa*—e.g., of Corelli—has four movements, alternately slow and fast. The instruments are typically two violins with accompanying harpsichord and string bass.

Choir
A body of voices, probably twelve or more. The term used to be reserved for church singers, but this is no longer the case.

Chorale
A church song or hymn. The term is usually applied to German Lutheran hymn tunes such as feature in Bach's cantata style. Occasionally it is used to mean 'choir'.

Chorale Prelude
An instrumental piece, usually for organ and based on a chorale melody, which is used as a **Cantus firmus**, the subject of a fugue, for variations (chorale partita) and so on.

Chord
The agglomeration of three or more notes simultaneously sounding and forming a harmonic unit. (Two notes only are usually called an interval.)

Choreographic Poem
An orchestral piece, like a symphonic poem only expressing a dance 'spirit', such as Ravel's *La Valse*.

Choreography
The art of composing dance movements for ballet; or the actual sequence of dance movements in a particular balletic work.

Chorus
A body of voices, usually not connected with a church; or a choral item in an opera, oratorio etc.

Chromatic
Literally 'coloured'. Chromatic notes in melody are those not belonging to the key in the context of which they are used, and a chromatic chord also contains one or more notes of this kind. The chromatic scale is that which includes all twelve semitones of the octave.

Circle of Fifths
Starting with C, the major keys in a sequence of ascending perfect fifths (C, G, D, A, E etc) have successively one more sharp until six sharps and F sharp major are reached. Going in the opposite direction (C, F, B flat, E flat, A flat etc) we find that the number of flats increases in the same way. The two 'directions' in fact meet at F sharp major/G flat major which has six sharps or six flats according to the chosen notation. Exactly the same happens with minor keys starting from A, the meeting point for both 'directions' being D sharp minor/E flat minor. It is worth noting that these exact meeting points only occur in the now universally-adopted system of equal **Temperament**. 'Just' intonation, with acoustically pure fifths, would produce anomalies.

Classicism
The so-called classical period from about 1750–1830, though short, was musically rich indeed, occupying the years between Bach's death and Berlioz's *Symphonie fantastique*. It includes the work of Mozart, Haydn, Beethoven and Schubert and is perhaps especially dominated by instrumental compositions from the German-speaking world, although Italian opera too (to which Mozart himself contributed) is important. This was the age of sonata form, of the growth of the string quartet, concerto and symphony, a time in which (as with the classicism of antiquity) form and order are idealized and achieved without the loss of human feeling in an art of maturity and enlightenment. It gave way, in the 19th century, to the more unstable and individual art of the romantics in which emotional self-expression might be a primary ideal

The chromatic scale

(Berlioz, Tchaikovsky etc). (Arguably, however, there are both classical and romantic attitudes to be found together at any point in musical history—the art of Palestrina for example belonging to the former style and that of his compatriot and contemporary Gesualdo to the latter.)

Clausula
Literally, a cadence: but the term is used for short polyphonic compositions of the Notre Dame School in the 12th and 13th centuries, based on plainchant.

Clavier
Keyboard, hence also a keyboard instrument.

Clef
A symbol placed on the stave to indicate the pitch of the notes. The treble (or G) clef and the bass clef are commonest of all; the alto clef is used for the viola and the tenor is tenor-range passages for bassoon, trombone and cello. In older music, up to Bach's time, other C clefs (which like the alto and tenor show the position of the note middle C) were used, but these are now obsolete.

Clefs (left to right): treble, bass, alto, tenor

Coda
A closing section to a movement. In sonata form, it follows the recapitulation (assuming that a coda is used at all). It may be brief or, as in the case of Beethoven's 'Eroica' first movement, substantial.

Codetta
A short coda-like passage at the end of a section such as the exposition of a sonata-form movement. Also, in the exposition of a fugue, a linking passage between entries.

Col legno
'With the wood', of the bow of a stringed instrument: tapping the strings of a violin, etc., with the bow-stick instead of the hair.

Colla parte
Literally, 'with the part'. A direction to the accompanist to follow a solo line carefully in a freely-played passage. *Colla voce*, if the solo is vocal, is an instruction to follow the voice.

Con sordino
With the **Mute**.

Compass
The range of notes of a voice or instrument.

Composition
The art of inventing music. Also another term for a musical work.

Compound Time
A time—i.e., pattern of beats—in which the beat is a dotted note—e.g., 6/4, 9/8.

Computer
An electronic calculating machine. Advances in computer technology since about 1950 have been rapid, and sophisticated equipment today performs in some ways like a human brain. Where musical events are capable of being described numerically and so supplied to such a computer, a magnetic tape can be produced and played back. The application of random number generators may also give results unobtainable by other means. Computers can also be used for

style analysis, by programming informa-
tion on existing music.

Con

With—thus, *con brio* means 'with spirit',
con sordino, 'with the mute', etc.

Concert

A public musical performance. Usually
applied to orchestral and other groups of
performers; a solo performance is better
described as a recital.

*(Below) An open-air European concert in
the 18th century*

Concertante

'In concerto style', applying to solo passages in an orchestral work. A *sinfonia concertante* (such as Mozart's of 1779 for violin, viola and orchestra) is an orchestral work including individual solo parts but not to the same extent as a concerto.

Concertato

A term used of instruments playing

together. This Italian word can mean 'in agreement', and in baroque music sometimes denotes a style where different instrumental and vocal groups are combined and contrasted.

Concertino

A small group of soloists in an orchestral work such as a **Concerto grosso**. Or a small-scale concerto—e.g., Weber's Concertino (1811) for clarinet and orchestra.

Concertmaster

The leader of an orchestra—i.e., the first violinist. His role includes the performance of solo passages and sometimes advising a conductor on string bowings.

Concerto

A work for solo instrument with orchestra, usually in three movements. Occasionally we meet a double concerto (such as Brahms's for violin and cello) or a triple concerto (Beethoven's for violin, cello and piano), but these are the exceptions. Also exceptional is the use of four movements, as in Brahms's Second Piano Concerto. The form grew up in the baroque period (with Vivaldi, Bach etc) and reached maturity in classical times, perhaps above all with Mozart and Beethoven. With greatly increased virtuoso elements in the solo part, it served the romantics of the 19th century equally well (Mendelssohn, Tchaikovsky etc); and indeed most modern composers also have written concertos. It is clear that the appeal of the form—for composers, performers and audiences alike—remains strong even in the late 20th century. A 'concerto for orchestra', such as those by Bartók and Tippett, has no single soloist but offers virtuoso opportunities to the individual orchestral players.

Concerto grosso

An orchestral work of baroque times. Commonly two violins and bass (cello and keyboard) were set as the **Concertino** element against the remainder of the orchestra, called **Ripieno** or **Tutti**, consisting of strings and sometimes also wind. The *concerti grossi* of Corelli and Handel have four or five movements, those by Bach sometimes less—e.g. all but No 1 of the six 'Brandenburg' Concertos. Vivaldi also preferred the three-movement form, which incidentally anticipates the classical concerto of Mozart's time.

Concord

A subjective term for a chord that is pleasing and consonant to the ear; the opposite of discord. In practice the term is commonly reserved for triads, (e.g., C, E, G) since even a familiar and agreeable dissonance like a dominant 7th (C, E, G, B flat) is by its nature unsatisfying alone, requiring resolution on to a triadic chord, in this case F, A, C. It goes without saying that in non-traditional systems of composition such as Schoenberg's serial technique, the above (and indeed the whole concept of harmonic concord and discord) cannot apply.

Concrete Music

Musique concrète is the usual term, at least in Europe, for the style originated in France around 1948. The raw material of its sounds is not that made by ordinary musical instruments, but rather noises of various sorts, subjected at times to modification from magnetic tape recording (playing backwards, slowing down or speeding up, reverberation etc.). The 'concrete' element of the name, which in French sounds less 'way out' than it does in English, refers to the reality of natural sounds as opposed to the artificial nature of those produced by manufactured instruments. Perhaps the best-known work in this idiom is Pierre Schaeffer's *Symphonie pour un homme seul*, where ten short movements represent the sounds that might be heard by a man walking alone at night. Pierre Henry's *Vocalise* is entirely constructed from the variously modified sound of a single human voice singing the syllable 'ah'.

Conducting

Directing a group of performers. The conductor often holds a baton and with this he indicates the tempo and pulse (beat) of the music. At the same time phrasing and dynamics can also be shown by the nature of his gestures and even facial expression, the left hand being employed with a degree of independence. It is worth remembering, however, that a classical concerto—say, one of Mozart's for piano—can be directed from the keyboard by the soloist, as was done in Mozart's time and is frequently done today; and a small group like a string quartet is 'directed' largely by its first violinist.

Conductus

A medieval and early-renaissance vocal composition in which two—occasionally three—voices were added to a specially-composed melody. The style was fairly straightforward and chordal, possibly because, as the name suggests, there was a processional element. Some early solo songs to Latin words were also called by this name.

Conjunct Motion

Movement up or down the notes of a scale—i.e., by step. Movement up or down the notes of a chord is called 'disjunct'.

Console

The playing part of an organ—manuals, stops and pedals, but not the pipes themselves.

Consonance

Same as **Concord**.

Consort

A group of instruments. In a whole consort these are all of the same family—of viols, of recorders etc—while in a broken consort wind and strings are mixed.

Continuo

In baroque music, an accompanying bass line with figures indicating the harmony. It is normally played by string bass or basses and a keyboard instrument, the latter player filling out his part according to the harmonies shown. Sometimes

Pizzicato

Lusingando

Risoluto

Con delicatezza

The conductor's art of expression is uniquely and affectionately immortalised in these drawings by the late Gerard Hoffnung.

more players and instruments were used, according to the nature of the music. In some lighter orchestral music today—say in the musical theatre—continuo (i.e., chord) notation for keyboard players has reappeared.

Contralto
The lowest-pitch female voice, with a range of some two octaves with the E above middle C as its centre. The same as the female alto voice.

Contrapuntal
The adjective deriving from **Counterpoint**.

Contrary Motion
Movement of two melodic lines in opposite directions.

Contredanse
A lively dance style, and evidently a European name taken from the English 'country dance' of Queen Elizabeth I's court. Beethoven wrote some orchestral *contredanses* and used the theme of one of these for the finale of his 'Eroica' Symphony.

Corps de ballet
The main body of dancers—i.e., not the soloists—in a ballet company, corresponding to the chorus in an operatic troupe.

Cotillon
Dance of French origin, popular in the 18th and 19th centuries, to various kinds of music and with numerous changes of partner.

39

Counterpoint

The art of combining two or more melodic lines. In medieval music, the resultant harmony—individual chords and also chord progressions—was not a prime concern; but in Bachian and most later counterpoint a harmonic structure is all-pervading. Melodic and rhythmic shape are equally important in contrapuntal writing, where the ear must perceive the music both horizontally and vertically to absorb it fully: that is taking in both melody and harmony.

Countersubject

A melodic strand or phrase occurring together with the subject or answer in a fugue, probably first heard during the exposition in the first voice against the entry of the answer in the second.

Countertenor

See **Alto**.

Courante

A standard dance movement of the baroque instrumental suite, brisk in style and in triple time (3/4 or 3/2), sometimes heard as duple (6/8 or 6/4), perhaps because the Italian *corrente* had three beats to a bar but the original French *courante* only two.

Crab Canon

A canon in which the leading voice is imitated by the second voice in retrograde motion. Alternatively called *canon cancrizans* and retrograde canon.

Crescendo

Getting louder. Originating in vocal music, the effect was applied in instrumental pieces from the 17th century (Locke's 'louder by degrees', 1695) onwards and forms an essential part of the technique of composers as different as Rossini and Beethoven.

Criticism of music

The art of assessing quality in performing and compositional skills, usually in the form of the written word. All writing about music is critical in so far as it examines and analyses, and a scholarly work may criticise without the least element of censure or fault-finding. Indeed Stravinsky declared that to censure the composer's art for being what it was was as pointless as finding fault with the shape of his nose. Some composers have been perceptive critics (Berlioz, Schumann, Debussy) and so have amateur musicians like Hanslick and Cardus; while the literary skill and insight of George Bernard Shaw and André Gide make them also well worth reading. But Berlioz may have the last word: 'I have practically lost my belief that the critics can educate the public'.

(Below) The influential Austrian critic Eduard Hanslick (1825–1904) tells Wagner how not to compose (silhouette by Otto Böhler).

Crooning

A style of soft, rather sentimental singing, suitable only where electrical amplification is provided via microphones, used in popular swing music from about 1930 by artists such as Bing Crosby and Rudy Vallée.

Cross Relation

See **False Relation**.

Cross Rhythm

The simultaneous use of conflicting metres—e.g., 3/4 against 4/4—each bar (measure) taking the same time (but the speed of the beat differing) and the bar lines coinciding. Alternatively, the use together of conflicting bar lengths, say 2/4 and 3/4, with consequent independent bar lines for each rhythmic part.

Crotchet

The quarter note, written ♩ ♩

Csárdás

A Hungarian dance of the 19th century, in rapid 2/4 time. The word *csárda* means 'inn', especially a country inn.

Cue

In orchestral music, a short passage printed in a player's part after a long rest, showing him a recognisable passage played by another instrument immediately before his own entry.

Cueca

A fast-tempo, vigorous Cuban dance, with alternating 3/4 and 6/8 time. Bernstein's 'America' in *West Side Story* is of this type.

Cuivré

Brassy—a direction to horn players to produce this kind of tone. Sometimes indicated by a little cross over the note.

Cycle

A sequence—e.g., of songs—unified usually by a literary or programmatic theme. Schubert's *Die schöne Müllerin* tells a story; Britten's *Serenade* is a group of songs in which each poem has the theme of evening.

Cyclic Form

A structure unifying a multi-movement piece of music by the use of thematic material occurring at intervals throughout, or, by undergoing modification, forming the basis of the whole work. Examples include Berlioz's *Symphonie fantastique* and Franck's Symphony as well as Liszt's *Faust Symphony* and piano concertos.

41

D

Da capo
From the beginning. A direction to return to the start of a piece and play till the word *fine* (end) occurs, or some other such instruction. Commonly marked after the end of the trio section in a minuet to save writing out the first part of this A-B-A piece a second time.

Dal segno
From the sign. A direction to return to the sign 𝄋 at some earlier point in the music and replay from there to the end of the piece or some other marked point.

Damper
The felt-covered wooden strip which stops a piano string sounding when the key or right pedal is released.

Dance
The better-known solo and group dances of all countries and periods are dealt with individually in this book under their own names—from **Estampie** to **Rumba**. Dance for spectacle, as an artistic manifestation produced before an audience, is covered principally under **Ballet**. It is perhaps worth remembering here that dances provided a principal starting point for independent instrumental music, and such forms as the baroque *sonata da camera* and suite are essentially sequences of dance music.

Decani
In an English church, that part of the choir on the dean's side—usually the south side—of the chancel. (Opposite to the *cantoris*.)

Declamation
A style of vocal delivery somewhere between speech and song, more con-sciously pitched and rhythmical than ordinary speech. The same as *Sprechstimme* (**Speech-song**) as employed in Schoenberg's *Pierrot lunaire* (1912).

Degree
A step in a scale. Or a note of a scale—e.g., the mediant (the note E in C major) is the third degree of that scale.

Delicato
Delicately.

Demisemiquaver
A 32nd note. An eighth part of a crotchet (quarter note), written 𝅘𝅥𝅰 𝄽

Déploration
A lament, usually upon the death of a musician. Poulenc's Oboe Sonata of 1962 ends with such a movement and was dedicated to Honegger, who had died in 1955.

Descant
A melody line added above a principal tune, common in English hymn-singing as an added treble melody.

Development
An exploratory and expansive treatment of musical material such as occurs in the development section of a sonata-form movement. The techniques involved include key change (modulation) and the contrapuntal treatment of already stated themes or of shorter motives derived from them.

Diabolus in Musica
The tritone—e.g. F to B as a melodic interval in the key of C major. So called in medieval times ('the devil in music') partly because of its unique and disquieting sound, partly because of its sinister ambiguity. Acoustically it is nearly but not quite identical with the diminished fifth interval B to F (leading note up to subdominant) and thus reveals a curious 'flaw' in the harmonic system that puzzled and indeed shocked early theorists.

Diaphony
Two-part medieval polyphony of *c.* 1000: much the same as *organum*.

Diatonic
Pertaining to the seven-note scale—the major and minor scales, and also the older church modes. Used in antithesis to 'chromatic' and sometimes also to 'atonal' because of the association of diatonicism with the classical tonal system.

Diction
Enunciation of words in singing; verbal phrasing.

Diminished Seventh
The interval of the seventh such as occurs on the leading note of a minor scale—say, B up to A flat in C minor. Also the chord formed on the seventh degree of that scale—e.g., B, D, F, A flat. Useful in modulation (key changing) not least because it may be enharmonically modified (See **Enharmonic**). Thus if the A flat in the chord above becomes G sharp, the key of A minor is only a step away; and if the F becomes E sharp also, F sharp minor follows equally naturally. It is worth noting that the enharmonic changes still leave us with diminished sevenths, though not in their root position.

Diminuendo
Getting softer.

Diminution
The shortening of note values in a melodic phrase already heard, usually by halving them. A fairly common technique in fugue. Examples include Bach's Fugue IX in the Second Book of the '48', and the finale of Beethoven's Piano Sonata Op 110.

Dirge
Lament for the dead. A vocal or instrumental composition for performance at a funeral or memorial service.

Discord
A subjective term for a chord that is dis-

pleasing or dissonant—the opposite of 'concord'.

Disjunct Motion
Motion by leap in a melody line—e.g. up or down the notes of a chord as opposed to those of a scale (conjunct motion).

Dissonance
Same as **Discord**.

Divertimento
Most often, a type of 18th-century suite, perhaps for a smallish orchestra and consisting of several short movements such as dances and marches. But the term has been loosely used and includes much chamber music also. As the name suggests, a divertimento was music to amuse, in other words of an agreeable character. Modern examples include works by Bartók (for strings) and Berkeley (for small orchestra).

Divisi
Divided: a direction to orchestral string or other players to divide in order to play two parts. Usually abbreviated to *div.* and cancelled by *unis.* (unison).

Divisions
Baroque-period English term for the type of variations in which the tune is elaborated into quick running figures of shorter notes.

Dodecaphony
The **Twelve-note** system.

Dolce
Sweetly, gently. *Dolcissimo* is 'very gently'.

Dolente
Sorrowfully.

Dominant
The fifth degree of the major and minor scales, so-called because of its importance, second only to the tonic or keynote. In the old church modes, sometimes another degree, but this is now a rare usage.

Dominant Seventh
The chord formed upon the fifth degree of the diatonic scale by adding the 3rd, 5th and 7th above—e.g., G, B, D, F in C major or minor.

Dorian Mode
See **Modes**.

Dot
A dot added to a note adds a half to its value. Thus a dotted minim (half note) is equal to three crotchets (quarter notes). A double dot adds three quarters to the note length. In 6/8 time the beat is a dotted crotchet, and dotted beats apply in other compound times. (But note that these dots are immediately following the note: a dot above or below indicates **Staccato**.) A dot added to a rest has the same effect.

Double
A variation by melodic ornamentation of a tune already heard.

Double Bar
A double bar line marking the end of a section of music, or whole piece: usually the latter is distinguished by an extra thick final vertical.

Double Chorus
A chorus (choir) arranged in two separate halves so as to employ antiphonal—i.e., responsive—effects.

Double Flat
The sign which lowers a note by two semitones. It normally occurs only in flat keys—e.g., in a 'Neapolitan' cadence in A flat major. (See **Accidental** for illustration).

Double Fugue
A fugue with two subjects. The traditional scheme is to treat the first subject fugally, then the second, then finally the two in combination. Bach's G sharp minor Fugue, No XVIII in Book 2 of the '48', offers an example of this ingenious formal design. Alternatively a double fugue may at the start present a subject and countersubject simultaneously and treat them as a pair throughout.

Double Sharp
The sign which raises a note by two semitones. It usually occurs only in sharp keys: for example the leading note (seventh degree) of G sharp minor is F double sharp. (See **Accidental** for illustration).

Double Stopping
On the violin or other stringed instrument, the stopping of the string with two fingers to play two notes simultaneously. More loosely used, for the playing of two notes one of which is an open—i.e. unstopped—string.

Down Beat
The strong beat that begins a bar; also the conductor's baton or arm action to indicate that beat.

Drone
A sustained bass note or notes under a melody, also the low pipes of a bagpipe that provide such a bass.

Duet
A piece of music for two performers. Often, but not always, the two instruments or voices are the same. Piano duets are for two players on the one instrument. Operatic or other vocal duets are almost invariably accompanied.

Duo
For two performers, but not quite the same as a duet. It is sometimes the two-player equivalent of trio, quartet etc—i.e., a sonata or other substantial work for two instruments such as Ravel's for violin and cello. A two-piano ensemble is also referred to as a duo.

Dump
English instrumental piece of Elizabethan times (16th century), sometimes wistful in character though Shakespeare

*Mozart and his sister playing duets at the
keyboard, with their father Leopold; their
mother's portrait is on the wall. (Oil
painting by Johann Nepomuk della Croce,
Salzburg 1781)*

speaks of both 'sad' and 'merry' dumps
and the English word can mean many
things including a type of sweet, a small
coin, a kind of skittle etc.

Duple Time
Two beats in a bar—e.g. simple duple
2/8, 2/4 and 2/2, compound duple 6/8,
6/4.

Duplet
Two equal notes taking the time normally occupied by three.

Dynamic Accent
See **Accent**.

Dynamics
The 'volume of tone' element in music,
ranging from the softest *pianissimo* to the
most powerful *fortissimo*: clearly a highly
expressive element in the musical language. Dynamic markings, in order of
increasing loudness, are *ppp*, *pp*, *p*, *mp*,
mf, *f*, *ff*, *fff*. *Crescendo*, *diminuendo* and
accent marks are also common from classical times onwards.

45

E

Eclogue
An instrumental composition of idyllic or pastoral character. In French, *églogue*.

Ecossaise
A lively country dance in duple time, popular in western Europe between about 1780–1830. Beethoven and Schubert both composed piano *écossaises*. Despite the name, nothing to do with Scotland.

Eighth
The same as an **Octave**.

Eighth Note
The quaver, written ♪ 𝄾

Electronic Instruments
Instruments which produce their sound with the aid of electricity. Some, like the electric guitar, merely amplify sounds produced in the conventional way, and

The ondes Martenot, devised in 1928, was the first electronic instrument to feature in the symphony orchestra — e.g., in the music of the French composer Messiaen. It plays single notes and can also glissando between pitches.

the microphone, amplifier and loud-speaker may all be extensions of such an instrument. Electronic organs and synthesisers go much further, and here the sound is actually created by electronic means and reproduced through loudspeakers. The method is to generate a frequency corresponding to the note required and then to provide it with a tone quality by modifying its harmonics. Synthetic sound offers a rich resource, especially in popular music, for colour effects otherwise unobtainable. Perhaps the most 'classical' of electronic instruments is the *ondes Martenot*, first heard in 1928 and much used by Messiaen. Here the sound is produced by the 'beat' or oscillation between two high frequency sounds differing slightly in pitch, this beat itself being in the audible frequency range and heard as a note.

The American composer Milton Babbitt (born 1916) manipulates a complex of electronic sound-generating equipment as he builds up his music on magnetic tape.

Electronic Music

Music which is produced by electronic instruments. More importantly, the term especially applies to styles or techniques only available by this means. The modification of sounds in **Musique Concrète** is only made possible by the use of magnetic tape recording. Similarly the chance (random) elements of computer music are available only in conjunction with the computer itself. A wide range of new sounds is readily available from a synthesiser. So far the repertory of computer music and truly 'new' synthesised music—as opposed to the creation and performance of conventional music using synthesised sound—is small, but there is every reason to expect developments in this field. In the meantime a principle that seems to be evolving is that of 'the sounds themselves'—and perhaps also the technical resources—generating the structure of a composition. That is, the nature of the new musical syntax arises out of that of the computer itself. Since scientists rather than musicians design computers, this suggests a

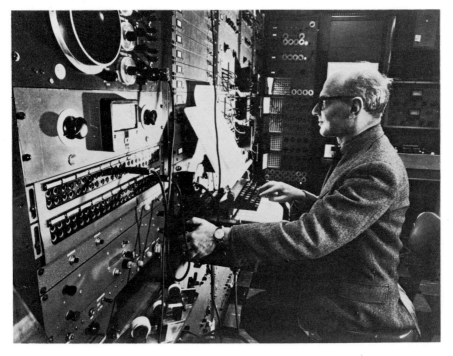

Electronic music in concert: the composer John Cage and his colleague David Tudor are in charge of the multi-tape mix which here constitutes the 'performance'. The music, called Rainforest, *emerges through loudspeakers placed about the auditorium, hence the informal positioning of the listeners, not all of whom appear equally absorbed.*

mathematical bias to such a new syntax, at least at present. But advances will probably be rapid, and it is unwise to predict the future.

Elegy
A sorrowful and lamenting composition, usually sustained and expressive in melodic line—e.g., Fauré's *Élégie* for cello and piano.

Embouchure
The lip position in the playing of wind instruments, particularly the flute and the brass family.

Encore
At the end of a concert, an extra piece not in the published programme and given only in response to audience applause. The French word *encore* ('again') is used in English-speaking countries to request such a piece, but in France the word is *bis*, the Latin for twice. Both of these words imply the same piece a second time: in opera this is what usually happens for obvious reasons, but in a recital the piece is usually something new.

Energico
Energetically.

Enharmonic
Properly speaking, pertaining to differences in pitch smaller than a semitone. In acoustical theory, using 'just intonation',

(*Above*) *Enharmonic modulation*

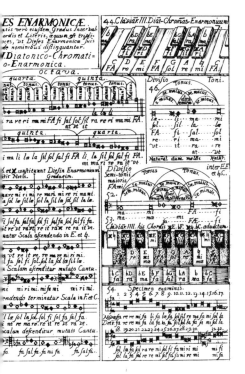

(*Above*) *The complexities of enharmonic change are illustrated in this page from J. van der Clot's* Notae Augustinianea *(1659).*

the pitch difference between G sharp and A flat (the lower) is of this kind, but as we know from the piano keyboard, in western music since baroque times (based as it is on the system of tuning called equal temperament) no interval smaller than a semitone is recognised and G sharp and A flat are effectively the same note. A key change from E major to A flat major using G sharp/A flat as a pivot is called an enharmonic modulation. The **Diminished Seventh** chord lends itself readily to enharmonic modification. Perhaps it should be added that a singer or violinist may nevertheless pitch the G sharp and A flat differently (though the pitch change is minimal) in the illustrated passage, and the resultant interval, just less than a quarter tone, between these notes would properly be called enharmonic.

Ensemble
A group of performers, as in chamber music. Also used to refer to unanimity in performance—tempo, balance, attack, phrasing style etc.

Entr'acte
An interlude, or piece of music designed for performance between the acts or scenes of an opera.

Episode
A section of a piece, particularly in fugue or rondo form, which separates statements of the fugal subject or rondo main theme.

Equale
A composition for a small number of similar voices or instruments. Beethoven's three *Equali* for trombones were later arranged for men's voices and played at his own funeral.

Espressivo
Expressive.

Essential Note
A harmony note: one belonging to the chord with which it sounds.

Estampie
Late medieval dance form of France, sometimes to words, lively in style.

Etude
A study, or even a pure exercise piece designed to improve a player's technique. It may or may not be suitable for a public recital—for example, no one

This medieval string ensemble including a hurdy-gurdy (or vielle, wheel viol) is entertaining the nobility above, at ease in their turreted château.

performs scales and arpeggios in front of an audience. However, concert studies, such as those for piano by Chopin, Liszt, Debussy, Rachmaninov etc, are intrinsically interesting as music and frequently played in public.

Exposition

The opening section of a fugue, in which the voices (parts) enter in turn. Also the opening section (discounting any purely introductory material) of a sonata-form movement, in which the first and second subjects are stated.

Expression

A subtle aspect of music and yet one of its most important. It is difficult to define since both performer and listener bring so much that is personal to the experience of the written notes of a musical score. An expressive composition seems full of feeling, while an expressive performance is one that conveys that feeling to a sympathetic listener. The quality is hard to convey in musical notation (compare an actor's printed text which is similarly only a starting point for a performance) although dynamic marks and verbal instructions contribute. All depends much upon a performer's own insight and ability to communicate. For a singer, tone quality and diction are especially important in conveying the expressive content of the text; but tone quality is equally an expressive resource of a string player. Finally, the flexibility of rhythm called *rubato* is a powerful element in expressive playing.

Expressionism
A 20th-century term for music, borrowed from painters of the Austrian-German school such as Kokoschka, which seeks to externalise an 'inner experience'. Schoenberg's monodrama *Erwartung* (1909) and Berg's opera *Lulu* (1937) are examples of this sometimes lurid post-Freudian style.

Expression Marks
Indications in a score that seek to define the expressive content of the music. They include words such as *grazioso* and *mesto*—graceful, sad. Some writers would also include under this heading tempo and dynamic markings, *staccato* and *legato*, piano pedalling and string bowing etc. But arguably these are part of the score, like the notes themselves, whereas expression marks are verbal instructions that actually describe the music to the performer so that he may better grasp its expressive intentions and convey them to the listener.

Extemporisation
The art of improvising music, the performer inventing as he goes along. For obvious reasons, extemporisation is usually done by a single performer. As for ensembles, there is melodic improvisation in a jazz break, but this is held together by a non-improvised—i.e., prearranged—chord sequence. From this it will be seen that it is possible to have partial extemporisation only. In **Aleatory Music** also some element of free music-making is required from the performers—rather as the players of a game have freedom of choice within the existing rules. Such early masters as Bach, Handel, Mozart and Beethoven were all famous for their ability to extemporise solo. Today the art has been to a great extent lost, save perhaps among organists: even the humblest village organist must sometimes extemporise to fill in time during a service. The extemporiser's skill involves a proper balance between invention and repetition: without the one, the music will clearly be monotonous and without the other it may ramble in a shapeless way. An ability to modulate (change key) neatly and purposefully is highly desirable; and so is a sense of dramatic climax, of tension and relaxation that together give the music a narrative quality such as holds the listener's attention.

False relation

F

increase speed. The accompaniment features guitar and castanets. There is a fandango in Act III of Mozart's *Marriage of Figaro* and another in Rimsky-Korsakov's *Capriccio espagnol*.

Fanfare

A short bugle or trumpet flourish using the notes of the major chord, with military associations. More elaborate fanfares use several brass instruments, not necessarily all of the same kind, and are in effect short pieces of a ceremonial nature. Both Beethoven (in *Fidelio*) and Wagner (in both *Tristan and Isolde* and *Siegfried*) have incorporated fanfares into opera.

Fantasia

An instrumental composition in free style, either in no recognised form—e.g., Bach's *Chromatic Fantasia* for keyboard—or suggesting a brief flight of fancy—Brahms's *Fantasien* for piano, Op 116. Beethoven called his 'Moonlight' Sonata

False Relation

Alternatively, cross relation. This occurs when two versions—different inflections—of the same scale degree occur, one in each of two different contrapuntal parts, in consecutive chords. In the following example from Bach's B flat minor Fugue in Book 1 of the '48', the D natural-D flat of the upper voices produces false relation; but the A natural-A flat of the tenor, being in the same part, do not. The curious effect of false relation, commonly forbidden to students of counterpoint, is nevertheless occasionally used by baroque and classical composers.

False Relation

Falsetto

A singing style which is, as the name suggests, artificial, where an adult male singer pushes his voice up into the treble range, often for comic effect. A more classical use of falsetto is found in the alto singing of broken-voiced male choristers—e.g., in English cathedral choirs. It seems that the falsetto effect is produced by the vibration of a mere part of the vocal cords.

Fandango

A Spanish dance in triple time, or 6/8, fairly lively and with a tendency to

a '*sonata quasi una fantasia*'. Most fantasias are for a single performer. Exceptions include Schoenberg's for violin and piano, Liszt's *Hungarian Fantasia* for piano and orchestra and the Vaughan Williams *Fantasia on a theme by Thomas Tallis* for string orchestra, works so different formally as to bear witness to the freedom with which this term is used.

Farandole

A Mediterranean—i.e., Provençal, Spanish and Greek—dance to pipe and drum, possibly of Greek origin, in which the dancers form a chain and follow a leader. 6/8 time is usual. There is an example in Bizet's *L'Arlésienne* music.

Dancing the farandole (painting by Brueghel)

Fauxbourdon

A technique of adding a vocal part, or parts to a given melody, originating in England in late medieval times and later adopted in France. The 15th-century French style, with the melody in the top part, is exemplified in the work of Dufay and Binchois and was effectively a form of harmonization which avoided many of the asperities of earlier polyphony. Indeed the term *falsobordone* was used in the 16th century for simple four-part harmonizations of psalm tunes and the like. The term 'faburden' may also be met with and usually means giving a simple descant to the trebles in an English hymn while the tune is sung by the tenors.

Feldpartita
A piece for wind instruments in the style of a divertimento, perhaps for open-air performance. There are examples by Haydn, from around 1760.

Fermata
A pause, indicated by the sign ⌢ placed over a note, rest or bar line. Sometimes the Italian words for 'long' or 'short' (*lunga, breve*) are placed above the sign.

Fifth
The interval between two notes five letter names apart, inclusive—e.g., C–G. This is a perfect fifth. An increase by a semitone—e.g., C–G sharp or C flat–G—gives an augmented fifth; while a diminution by a semitone (C–G flat, C sharp–G) gives a diminished fifth.

Figuration
A pattern or near-pattern of notes, such as broken chords or less commonly scales, used decoratively rather than melodically—i.e., in some accompanying role.

Figure
A melodic fragment or motive, usually consisting of a few notes only but having a strong, recognisable character—e.g., the three trumpet notes that are heard over and over again in the Moderato second movement of Vaughan Williams's Sixth Symphony.

Figured Bass
The bass line, with figures indicating harmony, used by the player of a keyboard continuo part in baroque music and in some lighter orchestral music today—e.g., in the musical theatre.

Film Music
Music written to accompany the action of a cinematograph film. In the earliest days of silent films, music was played live to cover the sound of the projector. But even at this primitive stage the music was chosen (or improvised) so that its expressive style fitted the dramatic events occurring on the screen. Film music is thus the cinema's equivalent of theatrical incidental music. Many composers have followed Saint-Saëns's early example (1908) and composed for films: notable names include Richard Strauss, Satie, Honegger, Prokofiev, Shostakovich, Copland, Walton and Vaughan Williams. It is worth adding that highly effective film music has also been composed by specialists, less known in the concert hall—e.g., (in English-language films) Richard Addinsell, Malcolm Arnold, Nino Rota, Maurice Jarre, John Williams and Ed Welch.

Final
The principal note of a church mode, on which a melody in that mode ends, corresponding to the tonic (keynote) of a major or minor scale.

Finale
The last movement of a symphony, quartet, sonata etc—i.e., a multi-movement sonata-form work. Or the closing number of an operatic act.

Fingerboard
The wooden strip on a violin or other stringed instrument against which the player's fingers press the strings to 'stop' them, so altering their pitch by changing their vibrating length.

Fingering
The method of using the fingers in instrumental playing, or the written indications for this (numbers above or below the notes). For keyboard instruments, where the thumb is used, the numbers 1–5 are employed; strings and wind use 1–4 save for the rare occasions using the thumb (say in cello fingering), where 0 is marked.

First Subject
The first theme of a sonata-form move-

ment, appearing initially in the exposition and again in the recapitulation.

Flat
The sign indicating the lowering of a note by a semitone without changing its letter name or its position on the stave. (See **Accidental** for illustration). As an adjective, 'flat' may describe singing or playing out of tune, below correct pitch. Less technically, a 'flat performance' may simply mean one that is dull or un-imaginative.

Florid
'Flowery' style: ornamental writing, often though not exclusively for the voice, with rapid decorative figuration.

Flourish
A passage in florid style; or a brass fanfare.

Fluttertonguing
A technique of tonguing giving a kind of 'rolled R' sound, employed in wind playing. It is mainly used for the flute, but other wind instruments are also capable of it with varying degrees of effectiveness. Britten, in the *Dies irae* movement of his *Sinfonia da Requiem* (1940), requires fluttertonguing at figure 34 of the score from a full wind and brass section of 22 players. (But he later remarked to the present writer that some fluttertonguing instruments, such as the oboe, sounded uncomfortably like the sounds made by a comb played with tissue paper.)

Forlana
A dance, originally from the mountainous district of Friuli, to the north of Udine in Italy, characteristically in 6/8 time. Bach includes a *forlana* in his First Orchestral Suite; and Ravel writes a *forlane* in his piano work *Le tombeau de Couperin*.

Form
The shape or structure of a piece of music: its organization of themes, placing of climaxes, differentiation of textures etc. Form is the architectural aspect of music and, as a teaching subject, important in a composer's (and even a performer's) training. Individual forms —sonata, fugue, variations and so on—are dealt with in this book under their own names.

Forte
Strong—i.e., loud. *Fortissimo* means 'very loud'.

Fourth
The interval between two notes four letter names apart, inclusive—e.g., C–F. This is a perfect fourth. A semitone increase—e.g., C–F sharp or C flat–F— gives an augmented fourth, while a diminution by a semitone—C–F flat or C sharp–F—gives a diminished fourth.

Foxtrot
A lively dance in duple time of American origin (*c.* 1915). Uncommon in 'serious' music, though Ravel writes one in his opera *L'Enfant et les sortilèges* (1925). The Charleston of the 1920s is an offshoot of the foxtrot.

The foxtrot, danced in 1915 by Irene and Vernon Castle in Chicago

French Sixth
One of the **Augmented Sixth** chords.

Frequency
The speed of vibration of a note, which determines its pitch. It may be added that the frequency of a vibrating length of string or pipe is inversely proportional to the length—i.e., half the length, twice the frequency, gives the note one octave higher.

Fret
Thin metal or wooden strip (of which there are a number) fixed across the fingerboard of some plucked string instruments—e.g., lute and guitar—to mark the correct placing of the fingers.

Friss
The rapid part of two related Hungarian dances, the **Csárdás** and **Verbunkos**. Alternatively called—e.g., by Liszt in the Second Hungarian Rhapsody—*friska* or *friszka*. The slow section is marked *lassu* or *lassan*.

Frog
The ridge on the neck of a stringed instrument that raises its strings above the fingerboard—in England more often called the 'nut'. Both 'frog' and 'nut', confusingly, can also mean the device at the end of the bow by which the string tension is adjustable.

Frottola
Unaccompanied Italian choral piece of the renaissance period, fairly simple and light, with the tune in the top voice. A forerunner of the madrigal.

Fugato
A passage in fugal style—not the fugue form but its contrapuntal, imitative texture.

Fughetta
A short fugue.

Fugue
A contrapuntal form of the baroque and later periods. There are three not very clearly distinguished sections: the exposition, middle section and final section. In the exposition the voices (usually three or four contrapuntal parts) enter in turn with the **Subject** and **Answer**. In the middle section, the tonic/dominant area of the exposition is quitted for a freer key sequence and there are episodes that abandon the subject for other, perhaps related material. The return of the subject in the tonic marks the start of the final section, which may employ closed-up (telescoped) thematic entries in the technique called **Stretto**. Here, or earlier, other devices such as **Augmentation**, **Diminution** or **Inversion** may be used. **Double Fugues** have two subjects, triple fugues three. Of all composers, it is doubtless Bach whose fugues remain models of invention and indeed poetry. In the hands of others fugue form can savour of academicism and dryness, though there are fine examples from Beethoven's late period. Bartók writes a fugue of original design as the opening movement of his *Music for Strings, Percussion and Celesta*.

Full Close
The same as a perfect **Cadence**.

Functional Harmony
A theory chiefly developed by the German scholar Hugo Riemann (1849–1919), which seeks to explain harmonic progression wholly in terms of the three principal chords of a key: tonic, dominant and subdominant (I, V and IV). The theory has been influential in the German-speaking countries, less so elsewhere.

Fundamental
The lowest note of a chord—i.e., the bass. Or the root of a chord, even when it is in inversion—e.g., the note C in reference to the triad E, G, C or G, C, E as well as C, E, G. In acoustics, the first note of a harmonic series, corresponding to the whole length of a vibrating medium.

Futurism
An Italian artistic movement originating with the writer Filippo Tommaso

Marinetti (1876–1944) who advocated new methods in all the arts—including cookery, where his *Cucina futurista* of 1932 suggested such recipes as *salame* sausage in a mixture of black coffee and eau-de-Cologne. His musical disciple, Francesco Pratella, imagined in 1912 orchestras of noise-making machines 'of the factories, railways, transatlantic liners

. . . the victorious kingdom of Electricity', but Pratella's actual works (now nearly forgotten) are considered rather tame in style by those who know them. Indeed the futurist approach, rather like that of some contemporary composers in the electronic field, seems to have been concerned largely with novelty of sound rather than of compositional method.

Umberto Boccioni's caricature of a futurist evening in Milan, 1911

G

G.P.
General pause.

Gagaku
The classical orchestral music of the Japanese court; also some Chinese and Korean music for orchestra.

Galant
The agreeable, elegant *style galant* of 18th-century rococo music—secular, highly ornamental, often dance-like—is exemplified in the more playful movements of Bach's instrumental suites, in the violin music of Tartini, the harpsichord pieces of François Couperin and perhaps Pergolesi's opera *La Serva Padrona* (1733). Essentially, *galant* style is gay and light-hearted, sometimes even frivolous, but always in a sophisticated way.

Galliard
Cheerful 16th-century dance from Italy, which became widely popular elsewhere in Europe, sometimes as the second half of a pair of dances, the pavan and galliard, in a kind of forerunner of the baroque instrumental suite. In triple time or 6/8 (compound duple), featuring a sequence of five steps—in pseudo-English 'cinque pace'.

Galop
A quick dance, in duple time, German in origin and popular in the 19th century. The alternative name was 'galopade' or 'gallopade'; the German word for it, *Hopser*, is accounted for by its hopping step. Beethoven wrote a galop for a horse show and called it *Pferdemusik*, horse music. ('Galop' and 'gallop' are of course the same word.) The galop was often one of the dances in a quadrille.

Gamelan
An Indonesian orchestra, and also the musical style of such an orchestra, particularly those of Bali and Java, usually including tuned gongs, drums, flutes and the *rebab* (fiddle). Unlike much eastern music, Balinese *gamelan* is not improvised and must be carefully rehearsed. Its singularly subtle and beautiful sounds have influenced western composers, notably Debussy and Britten.

A Javanese gamelan, *probably photographed early in this century*

Gamut

Originally, *gamma ut*, a medieval term for the low G of the bass stave. Now used to mean the whole pitch range of notes available in music.

Gato

Lively Argentinian dance to the guitar, in alternating 3/4 and 6/8 time like the Chilean **Cueca**.

Gavotte

Stately 17th-century French dance, featured commonly in baroque instrumental suites such as Bach's, in quadruple time and almost always starting on the third beat of the bar.

Gebrauchsmusik

Music to be used: utility music. The term was perhaps coined and certainly given wide currency by Hindemith (1895–1963) in the 1920s for the 'practical music' (a far better name) which he composed for amateurs to play and enjoy. There is a large amount of 1970s ensemble school music, perhaps especially in England, which though not so-called

belongs to this same unpretentious music-making category, nearer undoubtedly to a game for the players' enjoyment than to concert-style performance.

General Pause

A pause in an ensemble piece in which all the performers are silent.

German Sixth

One of the **Augmented Sixth** chords.

Gigue

Very lively dance, originally the British 'jig'. It features in baroque instrumental suites such as those for keyboard by Bach, which commonly have a gigue as their finale. Six-eight time, or at any rate quick groups of three notes, is characteristic—as is the long-short rhythm for pairs of notes. It is perhaps safe to say that the gigue has more sheer momentum than other baroque dances. The *Presto con fuoco* finale of Beethoven's Piano Sonata in E flat major, Op 31 No 3, is a gigue in all but name and proceeds at a headlong pace. A more modern example is provided by Debussy's orchestral *Gigues*, of a uniquely melancholy character.

Giocoso

Humorous.

Giusto

Exact, precise, proper. Thus, *tempo giusto* means 'strict time' or occasionally 'suitable' or 'appropriate' speed.

Glee

Unaccompanied English secular male-voice composition of the late 18th and early 19th centuries, chordal rather than polyphonic, so popular as a style that numerous glee clubs existed whose members both performed and composed in this form. The Londoner Samuel Webbe (1740–1816) is the best known glee composer—he wrote over three hundred, but is otherwise not remembered. The derivation of the word 'glee' is still not agreed: it is variously claimed to be from the Anglo-Saxon *gliw* ('fun') and *gligge* ('music').

Glissando

Sliding. For example it is possible to slide from one note to another on the violin or trombone. The marking *glissando*, as a performing direction, can also tell a pianist to slide over the white or black keys in a rapid scale-like motion, or a harpist to brush his fingers over the strings in rapid scales or even in chords (where some adjacent string must sound the same note). Some scholars consider that **Portamento** is a better term for the artistic and expressive semi-slide between notes of a violinist or indeed a singer. A 'real *glissando*—e.g., on the trombone, can be deliberately vulgar and comic.

Gopak

Vigorous Byelorussian dance in duple time, of which there is a famous example in Mussorgsky's opera *Sorochinsky Fair*.

Grace Note

An ornamental note, written in small print. Its length (time value) depends on the context, and it may occur upon or just before the beat, where a principal note will be written. There may be two or more grace notes in a group, but they still have no 'official' allotted time value and must take from the preceding or following written beat. There are a few exceptions to this rule—e.g., in Chopin's piano music, where the use of the small-print grace-note notation may imply cadenza-like freedom or simply rapid figuration (as in the F sharp minor Prelude or Etude in A flat major, Op 25). But nearly always, grace notes are free, fast and light in style.

Grandioso

Grand, with grandiloquence: dignified and even perhaps a little pompous. The big D major tune of the Liszt Piano Sonata is so marked on its first appearance.

Grave

Solemn, and at a slow pace, heavy in style.

H

Grazioso
Graceful, dainty.

Gregorian Chant
The plainchant of the Catholic Church, named after that Pope during whose pontificate (590–604) it was collected and codified and who seems himself, as a keen musician, to have supervised this work. It is used for psalm singing, the *Kyrie*, *Credo* and much else in the service. The voices are in unison, unaccompanied, and sing with a freely flowing rhythm avoiding the suggestion of metre and indeed also any strong accents. Texts, originally Latin, may in modern times be in the vernacular.

Ground Bass
A short melodic phrase that is repeated in the bass throughout a piece, or section of a piece. A passacaglia, such as Bach's in C minor for organ, is based on such a 'ground' used for a series of variations, though in this particular example the ground is not kept quite exclusively in the pedal—i.e., bass—part. Purcell uses many ground basses (examples are the song 'Music for a while' or Dido's lament in *Dido and Aeneas*).

Gruppetto
An ornament containing several notes. Originally a **Turn**. But Debussy uses the term more freely in his piano prelude *Minstrels*, where the performing direction means 'the *gruppetti* on the beat'.

Guaracha
Cuban folk song, topical and sometimes mischievous in text and musical character, with an introduction followed by a faster section perhaps with a different time signature.

Gymel
From the Latin word for 'twin'. Gymel implies two-part singing in parallel thirds or sixths (England, 13th–15th centuries) and may also be used as a performing direction, like the modern word *divisi*, to show where the singers of a part must divide temporarily.

Habañera
Slow duple-time dance originally from Cuba, after whose capital city it is named. There are examples by Bizet (in *Carmen*), by Ravel and—in the piano pieces *La soirée dans Grenade* and *La puerta del Vino*—by Debussy.

Half Close
The same as an imperfect **Cadence**.

Half Note
The minim, written ♩ ♩

Halling
A brisk Norwegian dance in 2/4 time. Grieg includes a *Halling* in each of Books II, IV and X of his Lyric Pieces for piano.

Harmonic Minor
The form of the minor scale representing those notes used chordally in minor-mode music. The augmented 2nd interval that results between the 6th and 7th degrees—e.g., E flat–F sharp in G minor—is usually avoided in melody writing, and so also in the **Melodic Minor** scale.

C minor scale: harmonic form

Harmonic Rhythm
The rhythmic (durational) pattern created by changes in harmony. In a Bach fugue in 3/4 time, for example, there is commonly a pattern of chord changes which makes the placing of the bar lines clear to a listener without any accent on the so-called 'strong beats' being needed.

61

Harmonics

Harmonic series on the note C

Harmonics

The series of sounds of different pitch generated naturally along with any note produced by normal musical means. The low C of a cello, when played, acts in fact as the fundamental note of a series (see illustration). The higher notes correspond to the string (or pipe etc) vibrating not only as a whole but also in fractions of the whole. Thus the second harmonic is produced by the two halves of the string vibrating, the third by the three thirds and so on. It will be noted that the multiples of two give a series of octaves. The higher the harmonic the fainter it is, by and large. Nevertheless—and importantly—it is the relative strength of the individual harmonics that chiefly accounts for the difference in tone colour (timbre) between different instruments playing the same note. The oboe, for example, has a brighter tone than the clarinet because its upper harmonics are stronger relative to the fundamental. Alternative names for harmonics are overtones and upper partials.

Harmonics are used in string technique, including the harp and guitar. Playing the string (bowing or plucking) while touching it gently at the halfway point produces the octave above the open-string note, with a special somewhat flute-like tone colour. Such notes are marked with a little circle above the note.

Harmony

The art of using chords. This involves not only the building of aggregates of notes but also (and perhaps especially) the use of chord progressions which, in the traditional major–minor tonal system, form effectively the syntax of music. It was only with the clear establishment of the tonal system in baroque times that harmony became firmly organized. Bach's work, and Rameau's pioneering treatise of 1726, represent the state of thought at this time; thus Mozart and above all Beethoven inherited a clear and universally accepted language of music that had not really existed until about 1700. It is worth remembering that most un-cultivated music lacks harmony altogether, and there is some truth in the description of harmony as the mere 'clothing of melody'. Yet it is more than this: for example it opens the door to the entire realm of key, for without it modulation cannot take place. The large-scale structure, indeed the drama of, say, Beethoven's music is inconceivable without its harmonic dimension.

Harmony of the Spheres

An ancient Pythagorean concept having nothing to do with chords as such. It is common to western and eastern thought alike and imagines a relationship between the different manifestations of Nature, including music. In Cicero's time, for example, the seven known planets were thought to govern the seven notes of the scale; while the Chaldeans related the commonest intervals to the four seasons. (See also **Music Therapy**).

(Left below) Harmony exercise by Bruckner, for the teacher he chose when he was 33, Simon Sechter

(Below) Harmony, explained by the Italian theorist Gafori, around 1500

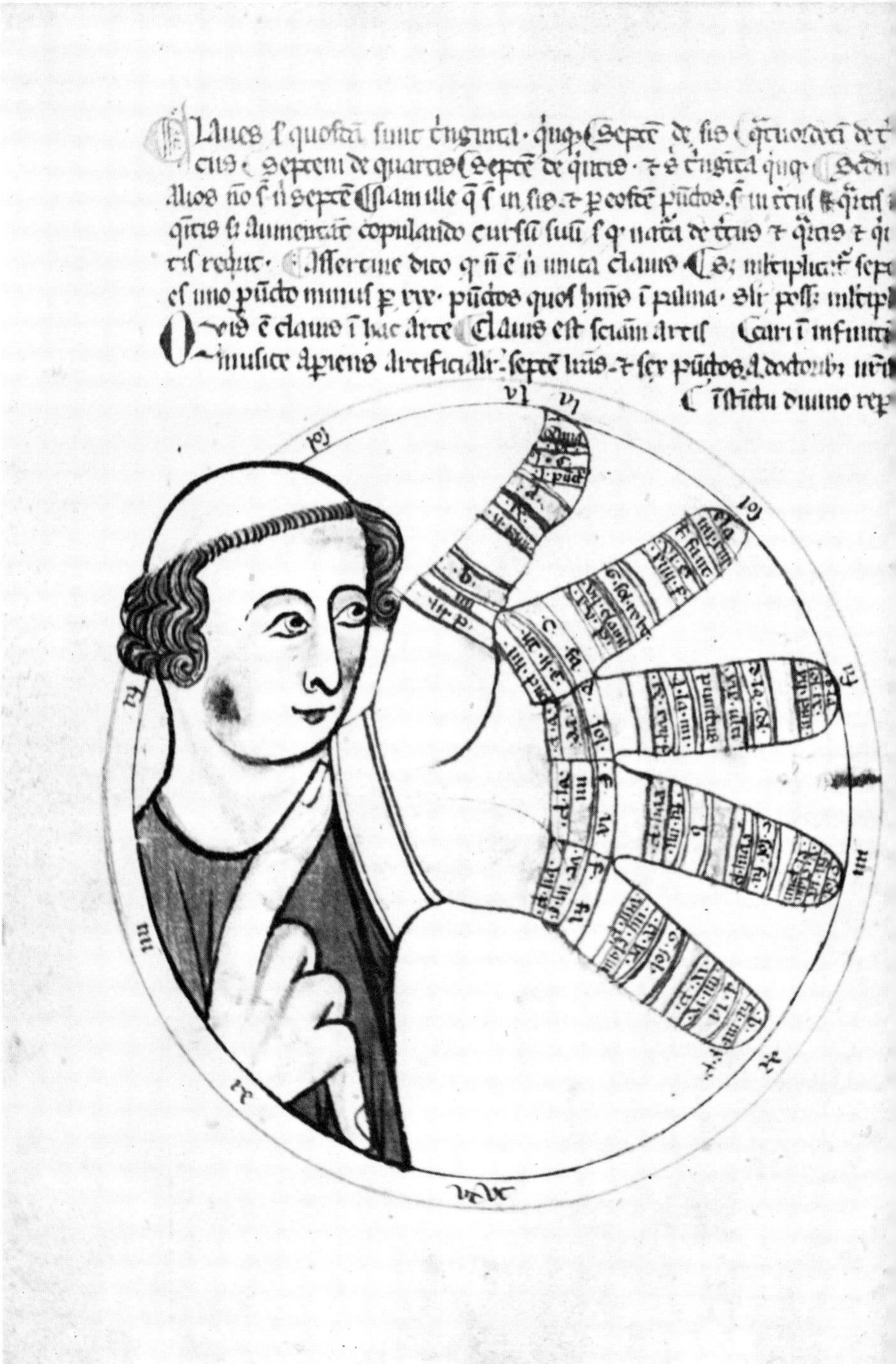

Hauptstimme
Principal part or voice.

Heel
The part of the bow of a stringed instrument nearest the nut or handle. Playing near the heel may produce vigorous, even rough tone and is marked *tallone* or *du talon*.

Hemiola
The term implies a 3 to 2 relationship. Commonly it describes the device of briefly changing from 6/8 to 3/4 and vice versa. It is common in the *courante* and also a favourite device of Brahms.

Heterophony
A loose kind of unison in which two performers play more or less the same notes, but part company briefly in the rhythm, by means of ornamentation etc. The effect is curiously antique and indeed the term heterophony is met with in Plato. Heterophony is a principal feature of the Balinese **gamelan** and plays its part in some of Britten's later works subsequent to his contact with Indonesian music.

Hexachord
A scale, not a chord: the same as the first six notes of the major scale. It was used by Guido d'Arezzo in the 11th century as a choir teaching aid, a sequence of tones (and in the middle, one semitone) which could be started at various pitches. The hexachord on F (*hexachordum molle*) involved the note B flat, the French word for flat (*bémol*) reflecting the old name. Incidentally this early transposition of scale patterns thus opened the way for the full range of keys available in baroque times.

(Left) The inventor of the hexachord, Guido d'Arezzo, also devised the 'Guidonian hand', a system of 20 points on the left thumb and fingers to indicate to his choristers the 20 different notes then available.

Hocket
A somewhat curious medieval device by which a melody, and its accompanying text, was shared between two voices in a chopped-up way. It was criticised as over-precious by church authorities and described as a 'ridiculous interception of the voice' by Abbot Aelred (12th century) or Rievaulx in Northern England. The French word *hoquet* means 'hiccup'.

Homophony
The opposite of polyphony, where voices or instrumental parts move 'in step' rather than independently. An English hymn tune in chordal style might be described as homophonic, compared to a fugue: it is essentially a melody with chordal accompaniment.

Homorhythmic
In chordal style, the parts sharing the same rhythm; more or less the same as homophonic. 'Rhythmic unison' implies the same thing.

Hornpipe
A brisk open-air dance of English origin, originally connected with a now obsolete reed wind instrument of that name mentioned by Chaucer. Very much linked with the sea and sailors, it is in duple or occasionally triple time. There are examples in both Purcell and Handel.

Humoresque
An instrumental composition, either of a good-humoured nature, as in Dvorák's famous piano Humoresque in G flat major, or perhaps of changeable mood, as in Schumann's more substantial *Humoreske* for piano. This latter piece was described by the composer as representing 'laughing and crying all at once'.

Hymn
A church song, nominally of praise to God but nowadays often having some other character—e.g., prayer for deliverance etc. The English hymn is choral and usually involves both congregation and choir, accompanied by the organ. There are other non-Christian 'hymns',

Rimsky-Korsakov's 'Hymn to the Sun' being an example, as are the surviving hymns to Apollo of the ancient Greeks.

A hymn to Apollo, and a funeral hymn, written on papyrus in ancient musical notation

I

Idée fixe

A motto theme which recurs in all (or most) movements of a large-scale work. It is Berlioz's own term for the recurrent theme representing the 'beloved' that features in various transformations throughout his *Symphonie fantastique*. In French *idée fixe* literally means a dominant, even obsessive thought.

Idiom

Style. To write idiomatically for an instrument is to compose appropriate music for it. Or a Spanish conductor might be said to give an idiomatic performance of one of his compatriot Falla's orchestral works.

Idiophone

An instrument that consists simply of material that produces its sound—a bell, castanets etc. An acoustical term: others similar to it are chordophone (stringed instrument), aerophone (wind), membranophone (drum) and electrophone (electronic instrument).

Imitation

Perhaps the most important aspect of counterpoint. A melodic idea (motive, phrase) is stated in one contrapuntal part and then in another, usually against a continuation of the first making a two-part texture; and the process may be continued with further entries. The imitation may be at the same pitch, or at the octave or some other interval. The entries of a **Fugue** and the device of **Canon** (both treated individually in this book) exemplify imitative technique.

Impressionism

The musical equivalent of the painters' art of Turner, Monet and others, rep-resented above all by Debussy (1862–1918). This is a music that avoids 'classical' clarity of statement in favour of an evocative and subtle style. 'Suggestion, not statement, must be the standard method; and things must be hinted, not said': the remark, made of the symbolist poet Mallarmé, fits Debussy perfectly. It was Mallarmé whose poem '*L'après-midi d'un faune*' inspired Debussy's famous orchestral work of the same name (1894): this hazy piece explores the mysterious world of waking dreams. The same composer's *Nuages* for orchestra was described by him as 'like a study in grey in painting' recalling Whistler; *La Mer*, really an impressionistic symphony, brings Turner to mind. Of course musical impressionism owes much to other musicians too, most obviously Wagner's later style as in *Parsifal*, and in its expressive intentions it is an offshoot of 19th-century romanticism. Debussy's impressionistic techniques (including his mastery of delicate, shimmering textures) influenced Delius, Falla, Stravinsky (as in the introduction to the second part of *Le sacre du printemps*), Bartók and Szymanowski, though this influence diminished sharply with the advent of neoclassicism after 1920. Debussy's great compatriot Ravel, incidentally, is only rarely impressionistic (as in the piano piece called *La vallée des cloches*) and it is incorrect to class him, as is sometimes done, with Debussy under this heading.

Impromptu

A short instrumental piece, nominally free as regards form but in fact often perfectly straightforward as in the piano impromptus of Schubert and Chopin.

Improvisation

Same as **Extemporisation**.

In nomine

An ensemble or solo instrumental piece from 16th- and 17th-century England, contrapuntal in character, that used as **Cantus firmus** a musical fragment of a John Taverner Mass setting that had the text '*in nomine Domini*'.

(Left) Degas's picture, L'orchestra de l'Opéra, *is highly impressionistic as regards the dancers, but hardly so for the musicians in the foreground.*

(Above) A courtly intermezzo *in the France of Henri III: the dancers represent the four virtues.*

Incidental Music

Music, usually orchestral, written for performance in conjunction with a play. If it is substantial it may well find its way, as a suite, into the concert repertory. Mendelssohn's *Midsummer Night's Dream* music, Bizet's for *L'Arlésienne* and Grieg's for *Peer Gynt* are notable examples among quite a large number of such works.

Inégales

In French 17th-century music, there was a convention called *notes inégales* in which a series of fairly quick notes, written as equal, were sometimes played unequally in a long-short pattern of pairs.

Instrumentation

The allotment of individual parts to instruments in an ensemble (usually orchestral) texture. Sometimes the term is used as a synonym for orchestration.

Interlude

A piece of music placed between other things, such as two scenes of an opera when the curtain is down—e.g., Britten's *Sea Interludes* from the opera *Peter Grimes*. The same, at least in the theatre, as an *entr'acte*. Britten also places an interlude for harp between the choral items of his *Ceremony of Carols*.

Intermezzo

As with an interlude, this is originally a piece of music played within some larger work. The comic interludes called *intermezzi* of 18th-century Italian opera were the forerunners of full-scale comic opera (*opera buffa*); and the French word *intermède* in Lully meant something similar, perhaps with dancing. In more recent times, the term intermezzo may simply mean a short instrumental piece: this is the way Brahms and Poulenc have used it.

Interpretation

Musical notation provides a detailed guide to performance, but it is not in itself the actual work, any more than a cookery recipe is the finished dish or an actor's script his performance. It is the musical performer's view of the score that constitutes his interpretation of it. It involves such matters as tone quality, articulation and speed, all of which may be indicated only up to a point in the notation. Even if the notation could be more detailed, there remain variable factors outside a composer's control such as the vocal timbre of singers, the instruments played (of which no two are identical), the room acoustics and so on, all of which affect performance. The performer's insight, judgement and personality must therefore always contribute, and though fidelity to the score is a *sine qua non*, those things which cannot be notated remain the performer's responsibility. No two performances, even by the same artist, are identical; and this fact of musical life illuminates the musical works themselves by constant renewal.

Interval

The pitch difference between two notes. Its size is expressed as a number, that of the total letter names, inclusive, between the two notes. Thus C to G is a fifth, C to A a sixth and so on. The separate intervals from second to tenth are each dealt with individually in this book. It may be worth adding that a few very rare intervals exist and may be met with once in a while. One such is the superdiminished octave B sharp to B flat found in Brahms. It occurs in the scherzo of his Second Piano Concerto, in the right-hand part of a solo piano passage of the trio section.

Interval: Superdiminished octave, B sharp to B flat

The same interval is used by Wagner in Act I, Scene 2 of his *Götterdämmerung*, resolving similarly inwards on to a minor sixth.

Intonation

Tuning: the art of singing or playing in tune. 'Just intonation' represents an ideal of accurate tuning that was superseded in baroque times by equal **Temperament**. The opening phrase of a plainchant melody, sometimes sung solo by the precentor, is also called its intonation.

Intrada

An 'opening piece', short overture or prelude, perhaps of a ceremonial character. The French term is *entrée*.

Introduction

An opening section, short or long, to a piece or movement, normally containing material that does not recur. A slow introduction to an *allegro* first movement of a classical symphony is common, perhaps especially with Haydn. Beethoven's introduction to his Third Symphony is a mere two chords, up to tempo; that of his Seventh (a slow introduction) is far more substantial. Brahms's First Symphony and Vaughan Williams's 'London' Symphony offer other substantial examples. The introduction to Tchaikovsky's First Piano Concerto is also of imposing proportions, indeed risking overshadowing the movement as a whole.

Invention

A term used by Bach for his short keyboard pieces in two contrapuntal parts (and now also applied to his similar three-part pieces) but otherwise uncommon. The word means little if anything more than it says—i.e., composition—and we sometimes speak in praise of a composer's powers of invention.

Inversion

Turning upside-down. A melody that is inverted has its intervals reversed, a fifth upwards becoming a fifth downwards etc. Invertible counterpoint means that the two parts can satisfactorily exchange places, treble becoming bass and *vice versa*. Triadic inversions are the two different arrangements of a three-part chord which place its two other notes in turn as the bass. As regards intervals, a major 3rd C–E inverted becomes a minor 6th E–C, and so on.

Inverted Mordent
See **Mordent**.

Invertible Counterpoint
Also called double counterpoint. See **Inversion**.

Ionian Mode
See **Modes**.

Isometric
Having the same rhythm in all parts, a similar term to homorhythmic and homophonic.

Isorhythm
A technique in which a rhythm is repeated, but not applied to recurring notes. A structural device of late medieval music—e.g., in the motets of Machaut in the 14th century.

Italian Sixth
One of the **Augmented Sixth** chords.

Jacara
Of Spanish and Portuguese origin, a 17th-century comic interlude inserted into stage plays. It developed into the 18th-century *tonadilla* of Spanish comic opera just as the Italian *intermezzo* developed into full-scale *opera buffa*. Later, a popular ballad or dance piece.

Jam Session
An **Improvisation** for a group of jazz musicians, usually on the basis of a well-known tune.

Jazz
The origin of the word, first met with around 1917, is obscure. Jazz is the principal American folk music of the early twentieth century, black in origin but using the instruments of white band music—banjo, bass, brass and other wind instruments, and later the piano, saxophone and so on. Scott Joplin's first piano rags came out at the turn of the century; 'Jelly Roll' Morton and 'Fats' Waller carried on the ragtime tradition of instrumental music, and it was later taken up by white musicians, notably the Russian-born Irving Berlin who composed 'Alexander's Ragtime Band' in 1911 and opened the way to the popular white big-band jazz of Paul Whiteman and George Gershwin in the 1920s.

In the meantime the vocal (as well as instrumental) blues idiom had emerged in the first decade of the century with Morton's 'Jelly Roll Blues' (1905) and W. C. Handy's 'Memphis Blues' (1912) and 'St Louis Blues' (1913) (see also **Blues**). Recorded jazz and the growth of an important musical industry in the 1920s meant greater earnings for musicians, and many who were academically trained came into this field and learned to

71

New Orleans jazz on stage: the trumpeter using a mute (centre background) is the young Louis Armstrong.

play idiomatic jazz, whether black or white. This was the 'Jazz Age' and that of 'Tin Pan Alley'—the title of a 1930 book by Goldberg. But jazz was already veering towards the smoother (and more white-orientated) style of swing, with its

(Above) Big-band jazz in the 1930s: Paul Whiteman and his Orchestra

elegantly presented large bands and sophisticated crooners. Later developments such as bop belong to the period after World War II. (See also **Swing, Crooning, Boogie-woogie, Bop**) Since about 1950, however, there has been a revival of interest in traditional or 'classical' jazz, especially in England where such musicians as Humphrey Lyttleton and Acker Bilk have sought to perform in the authentic style of the early jazz masters.

Jazz has influenced mainstream classical musicians. Stravinsky has written a 'Ragtime' and 'Piano Rag-music', Ravel a foxtrot and blues in the opera *L'Enfant et les sortilèges* and Violin Sonata respectively and so on. Kurt Weill, in his *Dreigroschenoper*, is close to the jazz idiom throughout though less life-affirming in spirit. In America, Copland and Gershwin (from similar New York–Jewish backgrounds) have also explored jazz style fruitfully; Gershwin's *Rhapsody in Blue* (1924), written for the Paul Whiteman Orchestra, is rightly famous. Most recently, in England Peter Maxwell Davies (b. 1934) has shown a nostalgic interest in foxtrots and other old jazz (or semi-jazz) styles that has proved important in his work. Another Englishman, Richard Rodney Bennett, has earned a reputation as a jazz and swing pianist that accords interestingly with his own somewhat 'advanced' and difficult composing style as an ex-pupil of Pierre Boulez.

Jig

An English Elizabethan dance, of the liveliest character, the original of the European *gigue*. Also an English low-comedy theatrical entertainment popular until about the 18th century. A recent theory suggests that jigs imitated by American black musicians influenced the dances of minstrel shows and later jazz itself.

Jongleur

A medieval itinerant minstrel of professional musical status but not of the social rank of the French troubadours or German *Minnesinger*. The name relates both to the Latin *joculator* and the English 'juggler', which together suggest that the *jongleurs* were all-round entertainers —comedians, acrobats and musicians all at once. The Italian poet Petrarch called them 'people of no great wit, but with amazing memory, very industrious and immeasurably impudent'.

Joropo

A Venezuelan dance song in fast triple time.

Jota

A rapid triple-time Spanish dance with castanets accompaniment, something like a quick waltz, from Aragon in north-eastern Spain. Glinka wrote an orchestral *Jota aragonesa* in 1845.

Jubilus

In early Christian plainchant (*c.* 400), a run of notes sung on the last syllable of the word *alleluia*.

Just Intonation
See **Intonation**.

(Left) Double pipe and castanets, played by medieval jongleurs: *doubtless the castanet player is also dancing.*

Kapelle

Usually a small court or private orchestra. A *Kapellmeister* may be an orchestral or choral director, though nowadays a conductor in Germany is called a *Dirigent*.

Key

A hard word to define. Dating from about the 17th century, when it superseded the earlier modal techniques, the key system provides a set of notes related to each other of which the principal note is called the keynote or tonic. The notes of a key in classical western music are seven, and when played in order they give the diatonic—i.e., seven-note—scale, whether major or minor. Each note has its appropriate triadic (three-note) chord—the note itself, plus its 3rd and 5th—and these chords, singly and in progressions, form the harmony associated with a key, something of fundamental importance. Changing key is called **Modulation**. The notes of a key are indicated at the start of each line in a composition by a key signature of sharps or flats. The absence of either of these means that the music is in C major, A minor or written in a freely tonal or even keyless system.

The term 'key' also refers to the lever activated by a player in an instrumental action—e.g., of the piano with its keyboard or a wind instrument.

Key Relationship

The relationship between two keys. An important part of the structure of all but the shortest non-modulating pieces. Closest to the tonic are the dominant, subdominant and relative major or minor, together perhaps with the merely modal change from, say, C major to C minor or *vice versa*. The most remote key

75

from a given key is that with the widest difference in the sharp or flat direction, six steps in the **Circle of Fifths**—e.g.,C major and F sharp major, or F minor and B minor. Modulation to a remote key, particularly a sudden change of key, is a dramatic effect; the G major–B major switch at the beginning of Beethoven's Fourth Piano Concerto is such a passage.

Key Signature

The sharps or flats at the start of each line of a composition. These indicate the notes that are used: those notes not labelled as sharp or flat are uninflected—i.e., the 'natural' white notes of a keyboard. G major, for example, has one sharp on the

F line, showing the single sharp in that key. The minor key signatures correspond to the descending form of the melodic **Minor** scale—thus the sharpened leading note G sharp of A minor harmonies is not shown, and this key, like its relative major, (C major), has a 'nil' key signature. (See also **Circle Of Fifths**)

Keyboard

The range of finger keys of a keyboard instrument. On the organ and harpsichord it is sometimes called a 'manual', particularly if there is more than one. The word is also used to cover the various electronic keyboard instruments used in popular music.

Berg and Britten (at the start of Variation VI in Act I of his opera *The Turn of the Screw*).

Klavier
Keyboard instrument: in modern German the word is applied exclusively to the piano. (See also **Clavier**).

Krakowiak
A Polish dance in syncopated rhythm and duple time, named after the city of Cracow. It was danced energetically by large groups. Chopin's Op 14 is a *Krakowiak* (1828) in F major for piano and orchestra. Also spelt *krakoviak*.

Kujawiak
Or *kujiawiak*, *kujiaviak*, *kouiaviak*. A triple-time Polish dance, akin to the mazurka, that originated in the Kujawy district.

(Left) Keyboards old and new: grand piano (Roger Smalley) and synthesiser (Robin Thompson) join forces in an English studio.

Keynote
The tonic: the principal note of a key, after which it is named—e.g., C in C major or minor. The first note (degree) of a scale.

Klangfarbenmelodie
Not melody at all, but a series of changing tone colours, usually instrumental though possibly vocal, with or without the characteristic change of pitch level that constitutes melody as ordinarily defined. A term suggested by Schoenberg in 1911 for a technique already employed by him in the third of his *Five Orchestral Pieces* (1909). Literally, 'tone-colour melody'. Used also by Webern,

L

Lai

Medieval song form of France cultivated by the troubadours and (especially) *trouvères*. The poems are usually addressed to the Virgin Mary or other noble lady. The English word 'lay' is used very loosely by poets and others simply to mean a song.

Laissez vibrer

'Let vibrate'—e.g., a cymbal after it has been struck.

Lament

A 'sorrowing' piece: in Scottish bagpipe music an elegy for the dead, or an emigrant's farewell to native shores.

Lamentations

Latin words from the Bible (*Jeremiah*) sung as plainchant as part of the Roman Catholic service of *Tenebrae*. Later musical settings include those of Tallis (16th century) and Stravinsky (*Threni*, 1958).

Landini Cadence

A medieval **Cadence** named after the 14th-century Italian Francesco Landini, in which the sixth degree of the scale intervenes between the seventh (leading note) and the tonic. The effect is unlike that of a modern cadence because of the sequence of chords II–I (supertonic followed by tonic) and their disregard for the notes of classical harmony—e.g., sharpened fourths are often a feature.

Landini Cadence

Ländler

An Austrian country dance, as the name suggests. Probably the rustic original of the sophisticated, urban waltz. There are examples by Mozart, Beethoven and Schubert.

Largo

Broad, dignified in style.

Lassu

Part of the **Verbunkos**, a Hungarian dance consisting of a slow section (*lassu* or *lassan*) and a fast one (*friss, friszka* or *friska*).

Lauda

Usually in the plural, *laudi*. The *laudi spirituali* are devotional songs of 13th-century Italy, associated in particular with St Francis of Assisi and the Franciscan monks. They were solo songs without written accompaniment.

Lavolta

A late 16th-century dance of lively, daring character, in quick triple time. The name suggests the whirling around that was a feature. A painting exists of Queen Elizabeth I dancing the *lavolta* with the Earl of Leicester.

Leader

A conductor; or a first orchestral violinist (concertmaster); or the first violinist of a string quartet or similar ensemble. Alternatively, the initial contrapuntal voice in a two-part canon (leader and follower), fugal exposition etc.

Leading Note

The seventh degree of the major or minor scale, leading by a semitone upwards to the tonic—e.g., in a perfect cadence.

Legato

Smoothly played or sung, with the notes joined together, literally 'bound together'. A certain tonal evenness is also implied. Mozart said that a keyboard (piano) legato should 'flow like oil'. *Legatissimo* is the superlative. Legato may be indicated by the word itself or a **Slur**.

Leger Lines
The short lines added below or above the stave to accommodate notes lying outside the range.

Leggiero
Lightly.

Leitmotiv
A leading motive, as in Wagner's operas. It is a motto theme, usually brief, associated with some character or element in the drama. The study of the *Leitmotive* in the *Ring of the Nibelung* tetralogy is a branch of Wagnerian scholarship to which new material is even today being added: more than is generally realised, these musical ideas were developed and even combined in the latter part of the *Ring* and, strangest of all, they merge at times one into another in a remarkable way. Wagner's own term was *Grundthema*, 'basic theme', and the useful names given to *Leitmotive* are not his own but the invention of scholars.

Lento
Slow.

Libretto
The 'book'—i.e., literary text—of an opera.

Lied
Song: a German-language song such as those with piano accompaniment by Schubert, Schumann and Wolf. The term is usually reserved for romantic (19th-century) songs whose piano accompaniment approaches or indeed reaches partnership status. But the medieval *Minnesinger* songs and later German songs such as those of the 15th-century *Locheimer Songbook* were influential in forming the *Lieder* style.

Ligature
Notational signs of medieval and later plainchant that combine two or more notes in a single symbol. The forerunners of the modern grouping of notes that has quavers (eighth notes) joined by a single line, semiquavers (sixteenth notes) by two lines etc. Rarer uses of the term are (a) for the slur joining vocal notes sung to one syllable and (b) for the metal band joining a wind player's reed to the mouthpiece of his instrument.

Litany
In church music, a supplication—i.e., prayer—set to music.

Liturgy
The text (order) of a Christian service. Music for liturgical use is intended to be performed as part of the service.

Loco
'In place'—a word used to cancel the direction to play an octave higher or lower than written pitch.

Locrian Mode
See **Modes**.

Loure
17th-century dance, in moderate 6/4 time, perhaps originally accompanied by the bagpipe-like instrument of the same name.

Louré
A type of string bowing which has the notes slightly detached but played within a single bow-stroke—i.e., without changing direction of the bow.

Lugubre
Sombre, gloomy.

Lusingando
Coaxingly, persuasively, caressing in style.

Lydian Mode
See **Modes**.

Lyric
As an adjective, song-like, melodious, poetic in style. Grieg wrote numerous

short Lyric Pieces for piano. The noun implies a poem, or the words of a song, especially one in the more popular field. A lyric tenor is one of pleasantly light and melodious vocal timbre and singing style such as might be found in operetta. A 'lyric drama' is another term for opera, though an uncommon one. The word itself comes from 'lyre' and derives from the Greek.

M.D.
Right-hand—i.e., *mano destra* or *main droite*. Sometimes also used for 'musical director', especially in light music.

M.G.
Left hand—i.e., *main gauche*.

M.S.
Left-hand—i.e., *mano sinistra*. Also, manuscript—e.g., of a musical composition.

Madrigal
An Italian form of the 16th century, for a small group of unaccompanied voices perhaps in four or five parts. The words are secular, commonly about love or Nature—sometimes both at once. The madrigal came to England with a collection called *Musica Transalpina* in 1588 containing Italian madrigals with texts translated into English and also two by William Byrd. Subsequently English composers took up the form and it flourished abundantly for about forty years. The best-known English collection is called *The Triumphs of Oriana* and appeared in 1603, representing twenty-five composers in all.

The word madrigal was also used quite separately in the 14th century for two- and three-part secular vocal pieces—e.g., by Landini. Its origin is perhaps the word *matricale*, meaning a rustic song in the 'mother tongue', presumably dialect.

Maestoso
Majestic.

Maestro
'Master': a polite mode of address, in Italian and English alike, to a distinguished conductor or other musician. The French use '*maître*' similarly.

'The Four Singers' (attributed to Adam de Coster) are grouped as for a madrigal performance.

Maggiore

Major. Sometimes used to label a major-mode section of a piece following one in the minor.

Maggot

Old English word for 'whimsical fancy' and sometimes applied to light instrumental pieces in renaissance times.

Maîtrise

The choir in a French church.

Major

One of the two modes of classical western music since the 17th century, the other being the minor. A seven-note (diatonic) scale is used, and both melody and harmony are essentially formed from these notes, of which the first (keynote or tonic) is the principal. The scale is always the sequence: tone, tone, semitone, tone, tone, tone, semitone.

C major scale

Malagueña

Spanish folk style connected with the province of Málaga. Sometimes a type of **Fandango**, sometimes an intense kind of song.

Manual

A keyboard of the organ or harpsichord.

Maqam
Arab 'melody style' (plural *maqamat*).

(Below) An early masque performance at an
English wedding feast

March

Music for marching, in quadruple time, perhaps (but not necessarily) for military use. There is a 'Pacifist March' (1937) by Britten. And there is a triple-time march—a deliberate and humorous paradox—in Schumann's 'Carnaval' for piano.

Martelé

Heavily accented bowing of a stringed instrument. The Italian term is *martellato*—literally, 'hammered'. The direction is also occasionally met with in piano music for strongly accented passages. *Martelé* is marked with a kind of arrowhead.

Martelé

Marziale

In march style.

Masculine cadence

A cadence in which the final chord falls on a strong beat. The opposite is the feminine cadence, where the final chord falls on a weak beat or even between the beats.

Masque

A spectacular dramatic show of late renaissance and early baroque times, found in Italy and France (as the *ballet de cour*) but perhaps most of all in early 17th-century England, where Ben Jonson wrote masques for the Court. The music was only part of this extravagant form of entertainment, as were the text, costumes, elaborate scenery etc—rather as in a modern theatrical 'musical'. Milton's *Comus* (1634), with music by Henry Lawes, is perhaps the most distinguished work of this kind. The song 'Rule, Britannia' comes from Arne's masque *Alfred* (1740).

Mass

The Latin liturgy of the Roman Catholic Church for the celebration of the Eucharist. The *Kyrie*, *Gloria*, *Credo*, *Sanctus*, *Benedictus* and *Agnus Dei* are the parts that are traditionally set to music in a specially composed version. Some Mass settings—e.g., Bach's in B minor, Beethoven's *Missa solemnis*—are too large for performance as part of a service and are in effect oratorio-like works to be heard in their own right. The first known complete Mass setting by a single composer is that of Machaut in the 14th century.

Mattachins

A 16th-century dance by costumed men wearing stage armour. The same as **Bouffons**.

Mazurka

Polish dance in triple time, of varying speed, fairly free in rhythm, accented often on the third beat. Chopin's mazurkas (over fifty in all, spanning his entire career) are models and include examples of the varieties *kujawiak* and *obertas*. A few other composers have written mazurkas, among them Mussorgsky, Debussy, Scriabin, Szymanowski and Berkeley.

Measure

Same as **Bar**. Sometimes a dance, as in 'to tread a measure'.

Mediant

The third note of the major or minor scale—e.g., E in C major, E flat in C minor. So-called because it is half-way between the tonic and the dominant.

Medley

A pot-pourri of different tunes, usually in lighter—e.g., cinema organ—music.

Meistersinger

The word is usually plural and refers to guilds or societies of musicians, amateur song composers of the middle class, in late-renaissance Germany. Hans Sachs (1494–1576), the wise shoemaker of Wagner's opera *Die Meistersinger*, was a

(Above) In this medieval manuscript illustration a tonsured priest celebrates Mass. The Latin Mass liturgy of the Roman Catholic Church has inspired innumerable composers over the centuries.

(Below) A minor scale: melodic form

real person who wrote not only music but also poetry and plays. The *Meistersinger* had an order of seniority beginning with pupil (*Schüler*) and moving through three further ranks to master (*Meister*); they held regular meetings and competitions.

Melisma
A run of notes sung to a single syllable.

Melodic Minor
A type of minor scale that changes in its descending form, the sixth and seventh degrees being flattened by a semitone. The form of the minor scale associated with melody rather than harmony. (See also **Harmonic Minor**)

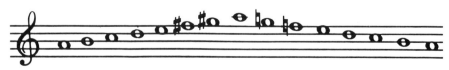

1 5 4 5 : HANS . SACHS N. ALTER. 5 I . IAR

(Above) Hans Sachs, the most famous of all the Meistersinger *in a 1545 woodcut: He is richly dressed and holds a manuscript; his age is shown as fifty-one. The strong hands suggest a craftsman, and the whole image is of a man lettered, benevolent and prosperous, as Sachs doubtless intended.*

Mélodie

Song: the word is the French equivalent of the German *Lied*.

Melodrama

Spoken text with music. Something of a rarity, though there are examples in Weber and Beethoven (*Fidelio*) and recitations with piano by Schumann and Liszt. Stravinsky's *Perséphone* is a large-scale modern work of this kind, though its composer in later years expressed reservations about the technique.

Melody

A sequence of notes (tones, pitches) forming a theme or tune. The rhythmic element is also important, and indeed a change of rhythm may totally disguise a melody. Many would claim that melody is the most important of all the elements of music. Certainly it is one of the most fundamental and (it has been said) the only musical element common to all peoples and periods. Harmony, for example, is relatively a very modern discovery and still by no means universally adopted.

Meno
Less.

Memory
Musical memory is of several kinds. We may distinguish between memory that is aural, tactile, visual and analytical: how the music sounds, feels, looks and (more intellectually) is constructed. In practice a performer perhaps combines some or all of these, though many would say that the first two are the most important. It is possible for a pianist to play a very familiar piece without consciously thinking about it at all: and here he is no doubt relying on his tactile memory in the same way as an industrial worker performing a familiar repeated action. Pianists since Liszt commonly give recitals from memory; but organists rarely do, nor do string quartets etc. There seems no especial virtue in doing without a score, save for appearance's sake. As for conductors, some use a score and others do not.

Mensural Music
Music in which the notes have a definite value, as opposed to the free style of plainchant. This 'measured music' grew up of necessity with polyphonic techniques in medieval times.

Mensural Notation
The earliest form of musical notation to indicate durations of notes and rests, initiated in the 13th century by Franco of Cologne with four lengths of notes—double long, long, breve and semibreve. The long could equal three or two breves, depending on whether it was 'perfect' or 'imperfect'.

Mesto
Sad.

Metre, Meter
The pattern of beats, indicated by a time signature.

Metronome
A device to emit regular pulses at a chosen speed, invented in Holland around 1812 by Winkel and then manufactured by Maelzel. The Maelzel metronome was a pendulum apparatus wound up by clockwork. Modern metronomes are more commonly electronic and can bleep and/or flash.

Metronome Mark
An indication of speed, given in the form of a note representing the beat—e.g., a crotchet (quarter note), and a number showing the number of beats to the minute.

Mezzo
Literally, half. *Mezza voce*, half voice—i.e., with restrained tone; *mezzo soprano*, female voice between alto and soprano; *mezzo legato*, half *legato*.

Microtone
Any interval smaller than a semitone. A very few western composers have employed microtones, among them being Ives, Hába Bloch and Henk Badings. Their use may increase with electronic music. (See also **Quarter Tone**)

Middle C
The C between the bass and treble clefs, nearest the middle of the piano.

Minim
The half note, written ♩ ♩

Minnesinger
German poet-musicians of the 12th to 14th centuries. 'Minne' means 'chivalrous love', but these courtly artists were perhaps graver than their French equivalent the troubadours. The most famous is

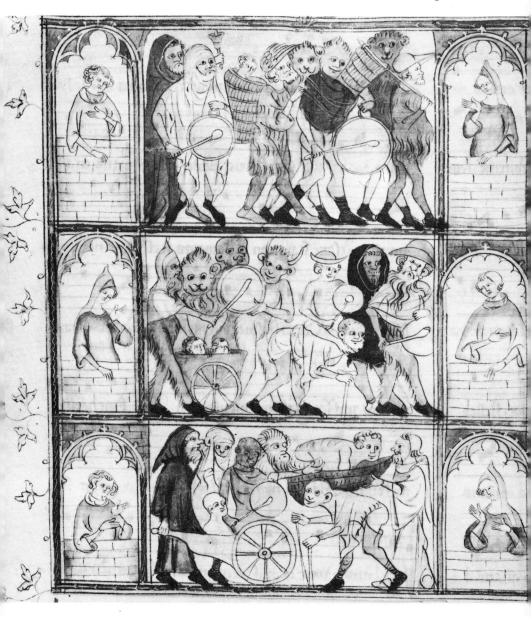

Walther von der Vogelweide (about 1170–1230). Their successors were the **Meistersingers**.

The travelling minstrels of medieval times were lusty entertainers and not simply musicians.

Minor

One of the two modes of classical western music since the 17th century, the other being the major. A seven-note (diatonic) scale is used and both melody and harmony are essentially formed from these notes, of which the first (keynote or tonic) is the principal. The two versions of the minor scale are illustrated elsewhere in this book. (See **Harmonic Minor, Melodic Minor**)

Minore

Minore. Sometimes used to label a minor-mode section of a piece following one in the major.

Minstrel

A medieval professional musician, an entertainer of the lighter kind. The French word is *jongleur*, the German *Gaukler*, while another English term is gleeman. The word minstrel has been revived in the last century or so—e.g., 'black and white minstrels'. (See also **Jongleur**)

Minuet

A European court dance of the 17th century, in an unhurried triple time. It became one of the optional movements of the baroque instrumental suite. Then, more importantly, it found its way into the classical symphony and string quartet as the third of the four movements, giving way eventually to the scherzo. The classical minuet is in ternary (A, B, A) form, the central section usually being called the trio section or simply 'trio'.

Mirror Canon

A **Canon** in which the second voice has either (a) the melody in retrograde (backwards) form or (b) the melody inverted (upside down). Or, a canon which is the same whether played backwards or forwards.

Misterioso

Mysteriously.

Mixed Voices

Men's and women's voices together.

Mixolydian Mode
See **Modes**.

Modal Harmony
Harmonic style, mainly of the 20th century, using the notes of the church **Modes**—e.g., a 'perfect cadence' with a flattened seventh (leading note) or a 'plagal cadence' in the minor with a major chord on the subdominant instead of the usual minor chord. A feature of Vaughan Williams's music, for example the *Fantasia on a Theme by Thomas Tallis*. It is worth pointing out that modal harmony does not represent a return to an older musical practice, since the modes were not harmonised at all in the modern sense.

The minuet as danced at Bath in 1794: from an aquatint

Moderato
Moderate speed.

Modes
The system of scales used in music up to about the 17th century. The modes of church plainchant and other early music were seven-note (diatonic) scales named after ancient Greek styles of melody which however have no known relationship with them. The principal modes of Pope Gregory's time (*c.* 600) were eight in number. The two principal notes of each mode were the final (corresponding to the modern tonic) and the dominant, marked respectively with an asterisk and a cross in the illustration. Four more modes were listed by Glareanus in the 16th century.

It may be added that a Locrian mode (with its Hypolocrian form), having the note B as final, was also considered but rejected because of the diminished fifth occurring above the final.

Modulation

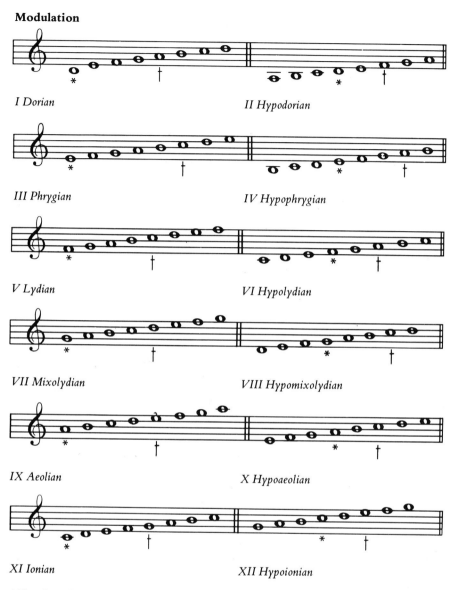

I Dorian

II Hypodorian

III Phrygian

IV Hypophrygian

V Lydian

VI Hypolydian

VII Mixolydian

VIII Hypomixolydian

IX Aeolian

X Hypoaeolian

XI Ionian

XII Hypoionian

(Above) Modes

Modulation

Change of key—established normally by a perfect cadence in the new key. The modulation is commonly approached by a pivot chord—one common both to the old key and the new—e.g., a move from C major to F major might include the D minor chord that is the supertonic in the first key and the submediant in the sec- ond; the chords of G minor, C major and F (the last two forming a perfect cadence in F major) would clinch the change. A dissonance such as a **Diminished Seventh** is also convenient for modulation.

Molto

Very.

Monodrama

A stage work for a single vocal performer—e.g., Schoenberg's *Erwartung* or Poulenc's *La voix humaine*. Or a **Melodrama** for a single voice.

Monody

Accompanied solo song of early 17th-century Italy, a kind of accompanied recitative—e.g., those of Caccini and Peri which begin the history of opera.

Monophony

A single melody line, as opposed to the two or more such lines in polyphony.

Monothematic

Based on a single theme. A fugue is mono-thematic; but a sonata-form movement, for example, is not. The finale of Mozart's Symphony No 39 in E flat major is monothematic.

Monotone

A single note, thus an avoidance of pitch change. It is common in plainchant, less so in later music, though Britten's *Rejoice in the Lamb* has a first section of eighteen bars of which the first thirteen confine the mixed choir to repeated middle Cs.

Mordent

A baroque ornament in which the written (principal) note is followed by the scale degree immediately above it and then the principal note once again. The inverted mordent does exactly the opposite—i.e., goes down-and-up. Unfortunately American and English terminology differs here. Some American authorities give the upper-note version as the inverted mordent and the lower-note version as the mordent. A safer nomenclature, in fact, is 'upper and lower mordents'.

Mordent

Morendo

Dying away—i.e. getting softer—and perhaps also decreasing in speed.

Moresca

A European 'Moorish dance' of the 15th and 16th centuries. The steps are not specified; rather, the name applies to the grotesque costumes and perhaps blackened faces of the dancers. The English Morris dance that survives today belongs in this tradition. There was evidently at one time a dance for two distinct groups representing Christians and Moslems.

Morris Dance

A successor to the **Moresca**. This English open-air group folk dance, for men only, has been known for centuries (it is mentioned in Shakespeare) and enjoyed a strong revival at the beginning of the 20th century. The dancers, sometimes with bells on their ankles, have colourful and varied costumes including ribboned hats and handkerchiefs, and may represent Maid Marian, a Fool, or ride on a hobby-horse etc.

Motet

Sacred polyphonic vocal piece, essentially the older equivalent of a present-day church anthem. It originated perhaps from the **Clausula** in 13th-century France and grew steadily in length and complexity. Among the masters of the motet are Josquin des Prés, Palestrina and Bach. During baroque times the form, previously purely vocal, acquired occasional organ or other accompaniment. The name of motet reappears at times in later music—e.g., in 19th-century France; and Vaughan Williams composed a set of three in 1920–21, of which only the first is unaccompanied.

Mosso

'Moved'. Thus *più mosso* means 'quicker'.

Motion

Movement of a melodic line or lines. (See also **Conjunct Motion, Contrary Motion, Distinct Motion, Oblique Motion, Parallel Motion, Similar Motion**)

The moresca, *as danced in Germany: the vigour and capering style may easily be related to the English Morris dancing that survives today.*

Motive

A musical idea, shorter than a complete theme, perhaps very brief or fragmentary. Even a rhythm, such as the 'three shorts and a long' that open Beethoven's Fifth Symphony, may be so described. An alternative word is 'figure'. Beethoven and other later composers frequently take motives from already stated themes in a sonata-form movement and 'work' them in the development section. (See also **Leitmotiv**).

Moto

Movement. Thus *con moto*, with movement—i.e., fairly quickly.

Motto

A theme or figure that commonly represents a literary or other extra-musical concept and that recurs in some significant way at various moments in a long work. The 'Fate' motives of Beethoven's Fifth Symphony and Tchaikovsky's Fourth are of this kind, and so is the D, S, C, H (D, E flat, C, B) personal motto of Shostakovich that appears in several of his works. The **Ideé fixe** of Berlioz is much the same, as indeed is the **Leitmotiv** in Wagner.

Movement
A section of a longer work, usually separated from other such sections by a pause. A symphony, for example, is usually in four distinct movements with contrasting speeds and keys—though the outer movements are both in the tonic. The movements are normally unrelated as regards thematic material, although important underlying resemblances may be sought by the analyst. Sometimes, however, the opposite is the case, as in Schubert's 'Wanderer' Fantasy for piano and Franck's Symphony, each of which has a main theme reappearing in various transformations throughout.

Murciana
A variety of **Fandango**, named after Murcia in Spain.

Musette
French type of bagpipe, adopted in court circles in baroque times. Hence, an instrumental dance movement of this period akin to the **Gavotte** with which it is often associated, featuring a drone—i.e., a sustained bass note or notes.

Music concrète
See **Concrete Music**

Musica ficta
Literally, 'feigned music'. In medieval times, the sharpening or flattening of certain notes in modal music, for reasons of style—e.g., avoiding awkward intervals. The accidentals were not always notated, but left to a singer's discretion.

Musica reservata
A 16th-century term first used to describe the music of Josquin des Prés, whose style was more harmonic in the modern sense than that of his Netherlands predecessors, and more sensitive also in the setting of texts. The choice of the word *reservata* (reserved, restrained) has not yet been satisfactorily explained, but we know that it was applied in recognition of at least two qualities—expressive setting of words in vocal music coupled with a sense of melodic flow.

Music Drama
The term used for Wagnerian opera.

Musicology
The academic study of music, applied to those aspects of the art which lend themselves to scholarship. Among the main musicological areas are analysis, editorial work, ethnomusicology (the study of folk music), psychology and aesthetics (where much remains to be done) and the sociology of music.

Music Therapy
The association of music and medicine. The ancient Greeks, and many other non-western peoples then and later, believed in the healing power of music, even associating particular styles with the cure of specific ailments like sciatica. A German book called *The Musical Physician* appeared in 1807, but it was not until a National Association for Music Therapy was founded in 1950 in the U.S.A. that serious modern work was done in this field. England followed the American example, and now music is used successfully in conjunction with other treatment, for example with autistic children. Some conditions of mental illness also have proved responsive to music. Finally, music has proved useful in the general rehabilitation of patients of all kinds.

Musique concréte
See **Concrete Music**.

Mutation
The word implies change. A mutation stop on an organ gives a note other than the expected one—e.g., a twelfth above. Referring to the **Hexachord** system, a mutation is a modulation from one hexachord to another. The break in a boy's voice may also be called a mutation.

Mute

A device for changing the tone of an instrument, muffling it in some way. Stringed instruments of the violin family have a clamp that is placed on the bridge, while brass instruments are muted by some kind of insertion into the bell (in the case of the horn, usually the player's hand). Timpani may be muted by a cloth over the skin. The grand piano 'mute' is a device operated by the left (soft) pedal that reduces the number of unison strings struck by the hammers.

Mystic Chord

An invention of the Russian composer Scriabin (1872–1915) consisting of fourths in their diminished, perfect or augmented form. It provides a harmonic basis in his orchestral *Prometheus: The Poem of Fire* (1910).

Nachtanz

An 'after-dance', the second dance of a pair—e.g., the galliard in a pavan-and-galliard sequence.

Nachtmusik

A serenade. Mozart's *Eine kleine Nachtmusik* is the most famous example.

Napolitana

A 20th-century music-hall song. Or any piece with Neapolitan connections, especially a **Villanella**. Also spelt *napoletana*.

Nationalism

A movement that began in the 19th century and survives in various forms in the 20th. The theory goes back to Rousseau and his pronouncement in 1768 that 'it is the accent of languages that determines the melody of each nation'. The use of folk material—dance rhythms, melodic styles, local instruments—is the characteristic feature of nationalist music. This began with Glinka in Russia in the 1830s; his successors, the so-called 'Five' (Borodin, Cui, Balakirev, Mussorgsky, Rimsky-Korsakov), carried on his work. Dvořák and Smetana in Bohemia, Grieg in Norway and later composers too—the Spaniard Falla, the Englishman Vaughan Williams and even the New Yorker Gershwin—are all nationalists to a greater or lesser degree. Vaughan Williams once said that 'Art, like charity, should begin at home. The art of music, above all other arts, is the expression of the soul of a nation.' In the years following World War I, nationalism came to be thought somewhat *passé*. Stravinsky, for example, seems to seek in some at least of his middle and late works to conceal the Russianness that was so apparent in his early Diaghilev ballets. But the emergence in the late 20th century of new countries, for example in Africa, suggests that here at least nationalist music will continue to appear for some time yet; while in eastern Europe and the U.S.S.R. ethnomusicology (folk music studies) is growing steadily in importance and already having its effect in the concert hall.

Natural
The sign indicating the restoration of normality to a note that has been flattened or sharpened. (See **Accidental** for illustration)

Natural Notes
On a brass instrument, those notes obtainable by breath and lips alone—i.e., without the use of the valves. These notes are in fact those of the harmonic series (see **Harmonics**).

Naturale
'In the usual manner'. Normally marked after a passage played in some special way—e.g., *sul ponticello* (near the bridge) on the violin.

Neapolitan Sixth
The first inversion of the triad on the flattened second degree (supertonic) of a major or minor scale—e.g., the chord F/A flat/D flat in C major or minor. It is an alternative to the subdominant chord that often precedes a perfect cadence.

Nebenstimme
A secondary part or voice. (The principal one is the **Hauptstimme**.)

Neck
That part of a violin or other stringed instrument that carries the fingerboard—i.e., not the body itself.

Nenia
A dirge. Brahms wrote a *Nänie* for chorus and orchestra.

Neoclassicism
A 20th-century movement that began as a reaction against the sheer size and self-conscious seriousness of late romanticism, against the 'hothouse' exoticism of Scriabin and perhaps especially against the increasingly personal and even autobiographical element in some music of the early part of the century—e.g., that of Mahler and Strauss. The positive qualities of neoclassicism lay in composers' search anew for the classical virtues of directness and economy, of freshness, humour and above all clear musical thought.

Prokofiev's *Classical Symphony* (1917) is perhaps a prototype, though in its deliberate simplicity it cannot tell the whole story. Stravinsky's *Pulcinella* (1920) is a more representative and influential neoclassical work, and still more 'serious' examples from the same composer are *Oedipus Rex* (1927), *Apollon Musagète* (1928), the *Symphony of Psalms* (1930) and the Symphony in C (1940). Vaughan Williams's *Concerto accademico* for violin (1925), which clearly takes Bach as its model, offers an English example. From Germany there is Hindemith's *Ludus tonalis* for piano (1943), with its twelve fugues and a postlude that is a retrograde form of its prelude. It may be worth adding that on the whole it is in instrumental music that neoclassicism has seemed to express itself most readily. Stravinsky provides something of an exception, yet even so, the stylisation of, say, his opera *The Rake's Progress* (1951) is perhaps something of an obstacle to the spontaneity and inevitability that one associates with undisputed masterpieces.

Neumes
The oldest notational symbols in western music. Beginning in the 8th century as little more than 'accent marks' showing the rise and fall of notes in plainchant, they developed over a period of centuries into (around 1200) the square notation used today in liturgical plainchant books. (See illustration overleaf)

New Music
From the German *neue Musik*, referring to 20th-century innovations such as Schoenberg's twelve-note technique.

*Aquitanian neumes, from a southern French
manuscript, probably 12th century*

Niente

Nothing. Thus *quasi niente*, almost in-
audible.

Ninth

The interval between two notes nine letter names apart—e.g., C up to the D
beyond octave C. This is a major ninth. A
semitone decrease (C–D flat or C
sharp–D) gives a minor ninth.

Nobilmente

Nobly. A favourite direction of Elgar's.

Nocturne

A night (or evening) piece of the 19th
century and later periods. Chopin's
twenty-one piano nocturnes are regarded
as the prototypes, though the nocturne
occurs earlier in John Field. Debussy's
Three Nocturnes are orchestral; and Brit-

ten's *Nocturne* is a song cycle in which all the poems have night as their subject. (See also **Notturno**).

Nodes
Points of rest or minimum vibration in a vibrating string or air column. These exist at the half-way point, at each third of the length, the quarters and so on. (See also **Harmonics**)

Nome
The ancient Greek *nomos*: a melody style or type, in the same way as such styles exist today in the Indian *raga* and the Arab *maqam*.

Nonet
A work for nine instruments, commonly in several movements as a quartet, quintet etc, and like them in sonata form. The best-known is that of Spohr (Op 31) in F major, for four strings and wind instruments.

Non
Not—e.g., *non lento*, not slow.

Notation
The art of writing music down. It began around the 8th century with **Neumes** and developed steadily into the present-day system. Notation is not universal in the musical world, however, and cultures such as that of India, where improvisation is a basic feature of music, prefer to do without it. But the ensemble works of western music, from piano duets to opera, can hardly dispense with notation, and indeed it grew steadily with the rise of polyphony. Even now, however, a composer's notation can never 'tell the whole story' as regards details of tone colour, *rubato*, textural balance and so on—hence the importance of **Interpretation.** (See illustration overleaf)

Note
A single sound of definite pitch (in English terminology); a key on a keyboard; the sign with which a single musical sound is written. Unfortunately, American and English terminology part company over this word: the first definition given applies to what in America is called a 'tone'. Furthermore, when an English musician says 'two notes lower' the American will say 'two tones lower'.

Note-Row
A series of notes used as a compositional basis in **Serial Music**. (See also **Twelve-note Music**)

Note Values
The relative values of notes indicated by symbols. (See also **Dot, Rests**.)

Notes Inégales
See **Inégales**.

Notturno
An 18th-century ensemble instrumental serenade. There are examples by Haydn and Mozart.

Novelette
Literally, a short story or sketch. Schumann used the term for his eight piano pieces, Op 21, and Poulenc has also written piano novelettes. The German spelling is *Novellette*.

Nowell
A carol—i.e., Christmas song. Sometimes spelt *noel*, as in French.

Nuance
A subtle shade, say of two-tone colour, dynamics or rhythm, such as gives unobtrusive expressive vitality to a performance.

Nuove Musiche
'New music', a term used for a radically new style of the early baroque (*c.* 1600) in Italy, which sought to give a vocal text a greater importance than in earlier polyphonic music and so tended to favour the accompanied solo song—i.e., melody plus a distinctly subordinate accompaniment—indeed more or less what is called recitative.

Nut
See **Frog**.

An early renaissance example of notation in a cordiform (heart-shaped) French song collection

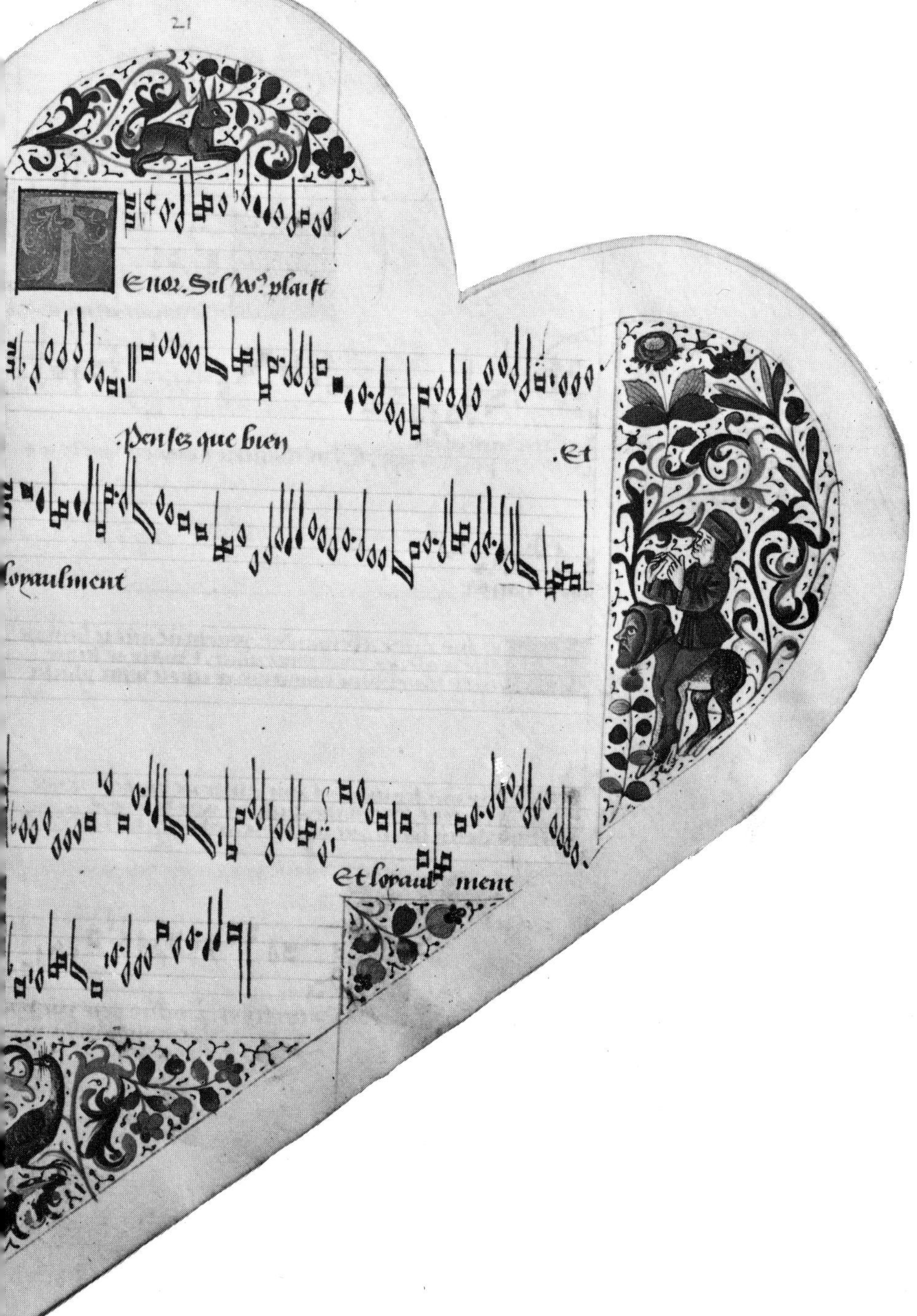
Pensez que bien
Et
loyaulment
Et loyaul ment

Obbligato

A term most commonly applied to instrumental solos that 'partner' the voice in an aria, frequently occurring, for example, in Bach's cantatas. Such an instrumental solo is of importance as a 'secondary solo'. Britten's song cycle called *Nocturne* uses seven different *obbligato* instruments, different instruments being chosen in turn to partner the voice—in one song, a duet of flute and clarinet.

Oblique Motion

'Movement' of two parts in which only one moves while the other remains at the same pitch.

Octave

The interval between two notes eight letter names apart, inclusive—e.g., C–C. This is a perfect octave. The augmented and diminished forms of the octave (C–C sharp, C sharp–C) hardly ever occur in practical music. The octave is the most perfect consonance; it corresponds to the frequency difference 1:2. (See **Frequency**)

Octet

A work for eight instruments, usually a sonata-form piece in several movements. Examples include those of Mendelssohn, Schubert and Stravinsky.

Ode

A ceremonial piece, in the nature of an address to some person living or dead. Purcell wrote a number of odes—e.g., for royal birthdays. Stravinsky's *Ode* of 1943 was composed in memory of Mrs Natalie Koussevitsky; while Schoenberg's *Ode to Napoleon* (1942) for reciter and orchestra, a setting of Byron's poem, is a far from complimentary address to the famous Corsican.

Open Fifth

A fifth—e.g., the note C with the G above. The 'openness' implies the absence of the third (E or E flat depending on whether the key is major or minor). To end a piece of music in this way is to create a bare and even harsh effect. The final chord of Vaughan Williams's Fourth Symphony is of this kind; and so is that of 'Mars' in Holst's *Planets*.

Open Strings

The unstopped—i.e., not fingered—strings of a violin or other stringed instrument.

Opera

Literally, 'works'. Opera is essentially a theatrical play in which the characters sing rather than speak and are accompanied by an orchestra. It emerged at the beginning of the 17th century in Italy, as an attempted revival of the spirit and style of the ancient Greek drama. By the end of the century, public opera houses flourished in Italy (especially Venice and

Troisième Journée.

Zauberflöte 1. Act.

Pap. *Der Vogelfänger bin ich ja,*
Stets lustig heißa hopsasa!

Dies tertius.

Rome) and the France of Louis XIV welcomed the new form, as did the great cities of Austria and Germany. In England, a centre of spoken drama and the **Masque**, opera did not take hold so readily, and Purcell's *Dido and Aeneas* (1689) remains an isolated masterpiece.

By the 18th century, however, opera of both the serious and the lighter kinds (see also **Opera Buffa**) was established in many European cities—including, since Handel's residence from 1712, London. Handel's work was in the classical **Opera Seria** style, with few ensembles or choruses, and texts dealing with the ancient world of heroes and gods. The Neapolitan operatic style of Alessandro Scarlatti (1660–1725) was at times rather lighter and placed great emphasis on vocal beauties and skills. The text (libretto) in itself tended to become unimportant in the 18th century, until the deliberate reform and rebalancing undertaken by Gluck in *Orfeo ed Euridice* (1762), produced first in Vienna and then as *Orphée* two years later in Paris. Mozart's operas, to both Italian and German libretti, mark a crowning point in classical opera, with texts that may be sophisticated or sublime but are never merely conventional.

In the 19th and 20th centuries opera has continued to attract composers. Some, like the Italians Rossini, Donizetti, Bellini, Verdi and Puccini, worked throughout their careers almost exclusively in the opera house; others, including Beethoven and Debussy, wrote one opera only but made it an influential masterpiece. Wagner's 'music dramas' are of towering stature; while in the 20th century we find a corpus of operas most obviously from Britten (1913–76)

(Above left) The cheery bird-catcher Papageno, in Mozart's opera The Magic Flute, *Vienna 1791*

(Left) The French baroque theatre of the 17th century provided a home both for plays (in this case Molière's Le malade imaginaire*) and for a rather grandiose type of opera such as those by Lully.*

(Above) Verismo *or 'realistic' opera:* Berg's Wozzeck *as performed in 1972 in Norway*

although most of the century's principal creators have written in the form.

Opera remains perhaps the most international of musical forms. Thus Stravinsky's *The Rake's Progress* (1951) has an English libretto by a naturalised American citizen, Auden, and had its *première* in Venice. Top-class opera singers must perform all over the world, perhaps in four or five different languages. But the high cost of presenting 'grand opera', with its requirements for a large stage, large casts, elaborate costumes and scenery etc, presents problems even in capital cities such as London, and subsidies are needed if seat prices are to remain realistic. Chamber opera, with a small cast and orchestra, may be artistically effective but is by no means the same thing. It appears, however, that the lavish productions of the Bolshoi Theatre in Moscow, The Metropolitan Opera in New York, or the Scala Theatre in Milan will continue for some time yet, not least because it is recognised that the quality of spectacle they afford consti-

tutes a national artistic asset.

Opera Buffa

Comic opera appeared in Rome soon after the birth of opera itself in Florence at the start of the 17th century. There were comic scenes in Landi's *Il Sant' Alessio* in 1632, for example, and a work called *Chi soffre speri* (Rome, 1639) was entirely a comedy. Later in the century Venice, with her several public opera houses, became a leader in this field. The most famous *opera buffa* of the early 18th century, and the oldest to survive in the repertory, is *La Serva Padrona* (1733) by Pergolesi: this work represents a tradition of two-act pieces with plenty of pace and humour (sometimes topical and satirical) and often brisk ensembles as final numbers to each act. The elements of intrigue that are also typical find their echo in Mozart's Italian comedies *The Marriage of Figaro* and *Così fan tutte* (actu-ally designated an *opera buffa*), though these works of the late 18th century go far beyond the simple Pergolesi model. (Mozart's German-text *Die Entführung aus dem Serail* was however called a **Singspiel** by its composer.) Works such as Rossini's *Barber of Seville* (1816), Donizetti's *Don Pasquale* (1843), Verdi's *Falstaff* (1893) and Britten's *Albert Herring* (1947)—together with the Gilbert and Sullivan Savoy Operas—are still in the same tradition of robust humour and bustle, together with tuneful music, that has always been characteristic. (See also **Ballad Opera**)

(Below) Good opera buffa *travels well even where its humour might seem local in character. Britten's* Albert Herring, *set in East Anglia, England, is seen here in a Leipzig production of 1968. The local Superintendent of Police (left) is, however, wearing a helmet that might cause raised eyebrows in Suffolk.*

Opéra-comique

This French term does not necessarily imply humour—the French have *opéra bouffe* for such pieces as Offenbach's —but rather a type of opera that has spoken dialogue instead of the recitatives of 'grand opera' and which is generally more homely. Boieldieu's *La Dame blanche* (1825), Auber's *Fra Diavolo* (1830) and even Bizet's *Carmen* (1874) with its tragic ending, all belong in this category.

Opera Seria

The 'serious' classical opera, exemplified perhaps above all by Handel's many works for the London stage in the early 18th century. The subjects usually concern heroes of antiquity or even gods. The name itself perhaps only arose to distinguish these works from comic *buffo* pieces. The style of alternating recitatives and arias, with few ensembles and choruses, eventually came to be thought distinctly old-fashioned. (Purcell's *Dido and Aeneas* of 1689, though profoundly serious in subject-matter, has absolutely none of the dramatic sterility of the Handelian *opera seria*, in which the music, including elements of vocal display, very much overshadowed the text.) It was these features which Gluck sought to change in his reforms (See **Opera**).

Operetta

A light piece of musical theatre, sometimes on the short side, not far indeed from present-day musical comedy, with spoken dialogue. The Viennese operettas of Suppé (1819–95) and the Parisian ones of Offenbach (1819–80) are prototypes. Strauss's *Die Fledermaus* (1874) and the Gilbert and Sullivan Savoy Operas (1875–96) are further examples from a long and often distinguished list that may properly include Leonard Bernstein's *West Side Story* (1957). Andrew Lloyd

(Left) Purcell's Dido and Aeneas *has all the tragic eloquence (but none of the dramatic stiffness) of the Handelian* opera seria *of a generation later. The production here is a modern one by the English National Opera in London.*

Opus

Webber's *Jesus Christ Superstar* (1970) and *Evita* (1978) are somewhere between operetta and 'proper' opera (the latter work is sung throughout and designated an 'opera') in a highly eclectic modern light idiom.

Opus

A work. Usually abbreviated 'Op'—e.g., Beethoven's Piano Sonata in C major, Op 2 No 3.

Oratorio

A setting to music of a Biblical or other religious text, presented as a dramatic narrative but with the singer-actors neither in costume nor 'staged'. Oratorio appeared in Rome in 1600 (exactly contemporary with the Florentine opera) with Cavalieri's *La rappresentazione di Anima, e di Corpo* in the Oratory of St Philip Neri's church—hence the name. This particular work was indeed staged, but the dramatic and spectacular elements soon fell away. Later oratorio composers have included Carissimi, Handel (whose *Messiah* is one of the best-known works in all music) and Bach—e.g. the *Christmas Oratorio*—though his **Passion Music** is best dealt with separately.

The Frenchman Marc-Antoine Charpentier and the Italian Alessandro Scarlatti take us into the 18th century, where C. P. E. Bach is also a significant figure, while around the beginning of the 19th century, Haydn composed his *Creation* and *Seasons*. Since that time, oratorios have been somewhat fewer. However, Mendelssohn's *Elijah* (1846) and Berlioz's *Childhood of Christ* (1854) are notable, as are Elgar's oratorios including *The Dream of Gerontius* (1900). A relatively late English example is Walton's *Belshazzar's Feast* (1931). Honegger's *Jeanne d'Arc au bûcher* (1935), with words by Claudel, is designated an oratorio.

Orchestra

The word 'orchestra' comes from a Greek word meaning a dancing place. Today it means a large group of instruments, as distinct from smaller chamber ensembles with only one player to each part. A modern symphony orchestra has

The Handel Festival of 1859, and a performance of one of his oratorios (with the usual vast chorus of the time) at the Crystal Palace in London

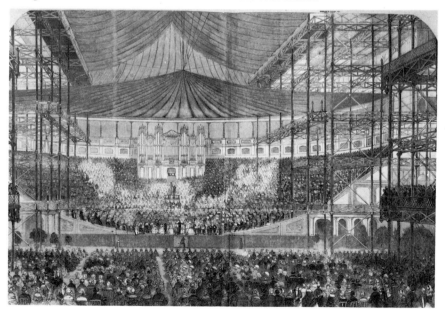

about seventy players of whom the majority are strings, where each part is played in unison by several players. The instrumental groups are woodwind, brass, strings including harp, and percussion.

Groups of players are known from the earliest times. But it was only in the 17th century, with the growth of opera and also ballet, that the nucleus of a standard body emerged. Later the string bands of France and Restoration England provided a firm basis. But Bach's six 'Brandenburg' Concertos (1721), each for different orchestral forces, remind us how varied orchestral writing might remain, and it was not really until the latter half of the 18th century, with Johann Stamitz and Haydn, that the 'standard' symphony orchestra was firmly established as a kind of 'instrument' for which a composer might write his symphonies and concertos. This is the orchestra of Haydn's 'Clock' Symphony (1794): two each of flutes, oboes, clarinets and bassoons, two horns and two trumpets, timpani and strings.

Since then, there have been various additions but no real changes. Instruments added in the 19th century include the trombones, introduced into symphonic writing by Beethoven, the piccolo, cor anglais, bass clarinet, double bassoon, tuba, alto saxophone and harp, together with the 'Wagner tubas' and various tuned and untuned percussion. The 20th century has seen the occasional use of the *ondes Martenot*, an electronic instrument of which Messiaen is fond. Keyboard instruments—piano, organ, synthesiser—also have an occasional place. But some popular instruments, like the guitar and recorder, are hardly ever used as part of an orchestral body, perhaps because their tone is insufficiently powerful.

Orchestration

The art of composing, or arranging, for orchestra. The term may best be used for arranging, (transcribing), say a piano piece; composers often prefer to talk of 'instrumentation'.

Ordre

A French word for a suite-like collection of pieces, used especially by Couperin.

Organum

The earliest form of two-part polyphony, known from the late 9th century. Originally the motion was entirely **Parallel**, but gradually there was more freedom, and eventually (12th century) there might be rapid runs of notes in the upper voice against a slower plainchant melody in the lower. This type was called 'St Martial organum' after the abbey of that name in south-western France where manuscripts in this style were preserved. (There seems to be no connection between *organum* and 'organ'.)

Ornaments

Decorative notes of all kinds, sometimes improvised, especially in baroque and rococo vocal and instrumental music, where such writing is fundamental to the style. (The word 'rococo' actually implies decoration.) The various written ornaments of music are dealt with in this book under their own names. (See **Acciaccatura**, **Appoggiatura**, **Gruppetto**, **Mordent**, **Shake**, **Trill**, **Turn**)

Ossia

'Alternatively'. Usually a passage so marked is an alternative, perhaps easier, version of something in a piece of music—e.g., a substitute for an especially high vocal note or a shorter cadenza etc.

Ostinato

Literally, 'obstinate': a repeated figure. Chopin's *Berceuse* for piano is based on such a figure, in the left hand, and *ostinato* figures are also common in Stravinsky, Holst and some other composers of the 20th century.

Overtones

Same as **Harmonics**.

Overture

Originally a prelude to an opera, oratorio, suite etc. Like the prelude itself, however, it has taken on independent life and concert overtures, having no connection with a longer work, are common. Mendelssohn's *Hebrides* is a famous example, and there are others by Berlioz, Brahms, Elgar etc.

P

Paean
A song of praise, originally to the god Apollo. There is an instrumental example by Arnold Bax (1938) for piano, later orchestrated.

Pantomime
Apart from the modern meaning of a Christmas musical show designed mainly for children, the word is virtually the same as 'mime'—i.e., acting without words, by gestures and expressions. Bartók called his *Miraculous Mandarin* (1919) a pantomime rather than a ballet.

Pantoum
This word seems, in musical terminology, to be a *hapax legomenon*—a word used only once. It is the title Ravel gave to the scherzo second movement of his Piano Trio (1914). The *pantoum* is a device of Malaysian poetry, which had been used by Hugo and others in France: it involves the use of lines from one stanza in different positions in the next. Ravel's wonderfully ingenious combination of two previously stated themes (one in quick triple time and the other in a slower quadruple) probably accounts for his choice of title.

Parallel Motion
Movement of two parts in the same direction without change of the interval between them.

Parallel Chords
Same as **Block Chords**.

Parameter
A mathematical term. When used in reference to music, it indicates such variable elements as pitch, dynamics and duration in serial and electronic composition.

Paraphrase

A reworking of an existing piece, more than an **Arrangement** and perhaps going further also than a **Transcription**. Liszt called his piano piece of 1859, based on a famous vocal quartet in Verdi's *Rigoletto*, a paraphrase. In a sense, a paraphrase is an elaborate and extensive single variation on an original.

Parlando

Literally, 'speaking'. A vocal style at the opposite pole from **Bel canto**, and suitable for **Recitative**, a 'patter song' etc. In instrumental music, the word (or *parlante* as Beethoven has it) implies simple, yet expressive delivery of a melody.

Parody

A work in the style of, or borrowing material from, some previous piece— e.g., the 'parody Mass' in renaissance times. There is no implication of mockery or ridicule.

Part

The music for a particular voice, or instrument. Or a single melody strand in polyphonic music. Also a section (usually substantial) of a composition—thus Mahler's Eighth Symphony and Stravinsky's *Sacre du Printemps* are both laid out in two 'parts' of this kind.

Partial

The upper partials of a note are its **Harmonics**.

Partita

An alternative name for **Suite**.

Part-song

Vocal composition for several voices, normally unaccompanied, but simpler and more homophonic than, say, a madrigal.

Pas de deux

In ballet, a dance duet. A trio is a *pas de trois*.

Pasodoble

A lively dance in 6/8 time, popular in the 1920s. Despite the name, a 'one-step' and not exclusively Spanish.

Passacaglia

A set of variations on a **Ground Bass**.

Passage Work

Brisk display writing of relatively little substance in a composition—e.g., flute or violin arpeggios, or even scales, over a principal melody. Similar to **Figuration**.

Passamezzo

Italian dance in duple time of 16th and early 17th centuries, similar to the **Pavan**.

Passepied

French (actually Breton) dance of baroque times, in triple time and both gay and light. Debussy writes a duple-time *passepied* in his *Suite bergamasque*, apparently in simple error. A common French spelling is *passe-pied*.

Passing Note, Passing Tone

A non-harmonic—i.e., dissonant—ornamental melody note, or more than one, between two that are harmonic.

Passion Music

A setting to music of the Crucifixion story as given in the Gospels, for church performance during Holy Week. Such settings are known from about the 10th century onwards and culminate in the two lengthy masterpieces of J. S. Bach, the *St John Passion* (1723) and *St Matthew Passion* (1729). In effect a kind of oratorio, a Passion setting of this kind has singers 'acting' the various characters, including Christ, while the chorus can be either the Jerusalem crowd or the pious modern congregation reflecting upon these events in hymns. An important German predecessor of Bach is Heinrich Schütz (1585–1672), whose style is far less elaborate yet still highly expressive. Handel and Telemann both set a contemporary poem by Brockes on the same subject. Stainer's still-popular *Crucifixion* (1887) is a more modern example, with an English New Testament text.

Pasticcio

A work by more than one composer. Not a straight collaboration, for usually each composes a distinct section or sections. Schumann, Brahms and Albert Dietrich composed such a Violin Sonata in 1853. A pasticcio can also be an operatic piece using existing music, perhaps with a new libretto.

Pastorale

A gently pastoral theatrical piece, instrumental piece or song. The old French *pastourelle* was a rural love song.

Patter Song

A song with rapid words, such as the 'Largo al factotum' in Rossini's *Barber of Seville*. There are examples too in the Savoy Operas of Gilbert and Sullivan—e.g., the 'Nightmare Song' in *Trial by Jury*.

Pause

The sign ⌢ over a note or rest indicates that it must be prolonged. Same as **Fermata**. No one has yet explained Schumann's use of the term for a short section of music in his *Carnaval* for piano.

Pavan

An Italian duple-time dance of stately character, dating from the 16th century, frequently with the **Galliard**. There are more modern examples by Fauré and Ravel.

Pavillon

The **Bell** of a wind instrument. The direction *pavillons en l'air* (found in Stravinsky's *Sacre du Printemps*, for example) means that the bell, in this case that of the horn, should be held upwards for maximum sonority.

Pedal

The word has several meanings: (a) the sustaining, soft or selectively-sustaining (third) pedal of the piano; (b) the 'foot' keyboard of the organ; (c) a foot tuning device on harp or timpani; (d) a sustained harmony note such as a **Drone**.

Pentatonic Scale

A five-note scale, such as is common to much ancient and other folk music from China to Scotland. The best-known of these is the scale C, D, F, G, A, in various transpositions, which corresponds to the black notes of a keyboard. The highly expressive Japanese *in* scale, on C, is C, D flat, F, G, A flat and lends an unmistakable flavour to music when it is used.

Perdendosi

Dying away, literally 'losing itself'.

Perpetuum mobile

An instrumental piece that proceeds in rapid notes throughout—e.g., the finale of Ravel's Violin Sonata.

Phantasy

A rather self-consciously literary spelling of fantasy (see **Fantasia**), adopted by W. W. Cobbett as the title for single-movement English chamber works composed for the Cobbett Competition that he founded in 1906.

Phrase

A small section of music, corresponding perhaps in literature to a single line of verse. Every melody seems to fall naturally into phrases, possibly because of a singer's fundamental need to breathe which may be carried over into instrumental music. Some scholars speak, not always usefully, of phrases, sentences, paragraphs etc in music; presumably a 'chapter' would correspond to a whole movement. (See also **Phrase Mark, Phrasing**).

Phrase Mark

A curved line, or 'slur', placed over the notes of a phrase to indicate its presence and extent. Not different in notation from a legato slur, though usually clear from the context: sometimes both occur together.

Phrasing

The art, in performance, of shaping music according to its phrase structure. It involves flexibility of dynamics (in which a phrase commonly rises and falls), of rhythm (**Rubato**) and perhaps also tone, all of which are matters that can hardly be fully notated and so are left to the performer. Skill in phrasing is a vital part of good singing and playing, and has been called 'one of the greatest refinements in the art of performance'.

Phrygian Mode
See **Modes**.

Piano
Soft, usually written *p*. *Pianissimo*, very soft, is written *pp*.

Picardy Third
See **Tierce de Picardie**.

Pitch
The height/depth aspect of a note—i.e., its frequency. Standard concert pitch is at present, for the A above middle C, 439 vibrations per second at 68°F. (about 20°C.). Older music, say pre-1800, is sometimes played at the lower pitch which prevailed at that time, especially when authentic period instruments are used. The actual pitch chosen is very much a decision for the performers, and may be as much as a tone down. (To complicate matters, it has been argued that while some of Bach's instrumental music sounded about a semitone lower

(Right) It is in Gilbert and Sullivan's operettas that we find some of the best-known examples of English patter songs. This picture is of the lively 'dealer in magical spells', John Wellington Wells, in The Sorcerer *(London, 1871).*

Più

than today's pitch, his organ music sounded a semitone or more higher!)

Più

More. Thus *più forte*, louder.

Pizzicato

Plucked. The technique of occasionally plucking the strings, when applied to instruments of the violin family, perhaps first occurred in a work by Monteverdi (1624).

Plainchant

The unison, unaccompanied liturgical singing of the Roman Catholic Church. Alternatively called plainsong. (See also **Gregorian Chant**)

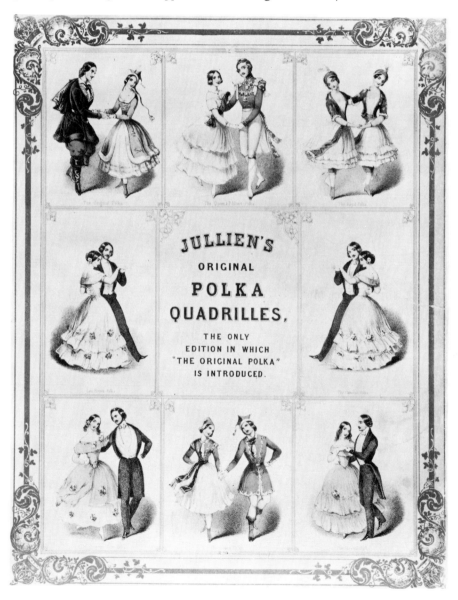

Poco

A little. Thus *poco più animato*, a little more animated.

Poco a Poco

Little by little. A *crescendo* is often so marked.

Poi

Then, next.

Point

The un-held further part of the string bow. At—i.e., near—the point (*punta d'arco*) is used primarily for delicate playing. Alternatively, an imitated motive in polyphonic music. 'Pointing' in Anglican chant means fitting the words to the music.

Polacca

Same as **Polonaise**.

Polka

Bohemian dance in quick duple time, introduced into concert and operatic music by Smetana—e.g., in *The Bartered Bride* (1866). Its lively 'hopping' rhythm is notably attractive.

Polonaise

Stately Polish national dance, or perhaps more correctly a kind of ceremonial walk, say at the beginning of a Court ball. Triple time and feminine cadences (ending on the weak third beat) are characteristic. The piano polonaises of Chopin have a heroic, sometimes tragic character. The *polacca* is another name, but the *polacca* in Bach's First 'Brandenburg' Concerto has little beyond its triple time to suggest the authentic polonaise style. With Chopin, the polonaise is perhaps the most 'national', in the sense of 'patriotic', of all national dances.

Polyphony

The art of combining melodic strands in two or more parts; also, music exempli-

(Left) The 'hopping' step of the polka is decorously illustrated in this title page from an 'original edition'.

fying that art. It grew in the vocal music of medieval times from **Plainchant** and **Organum** and has since been of importance as a technique of western music, although there was a reaction back towards simpler methods of musical expression in the 17th century—e.g., with the Italian **Nuove Musiche**. It may be added that polyphony is not usually a feature of non-western musical cultures, nor of folk music; and even now it remains for many people a learned, not to say arcane, branch of the art.

Polyrhythm

Rhythmic counterpoint. An excellent example (3/4 against 4/2) occurs in the second movement of Ravel's Piano Trio. The same as **Cross Rhythm**.

Polytextuality

The simultaneous use of different texts in a musical composition. It occurs in medieval **Motets** and is a feature too of operatic ensembles and the like.

Polytonality

The simultaneous use of different keys. **Bitonality** is not uncommon in 20th-century music. Three or more keys together are rarely found, as the polarising effect of two keys is changed into mere confusion. The composer Milhaud, who concerned himself much with these techniques, eventually concluded that, although fascinating, they were superficial compared with melody 'from the heart'.

Portamento

The technique, vocally or on a bowed stringed instrument such as the violin, of carrying one note on to another with a degree of 'sliding' between them. Used with skill, an effect that is artistic; otherwise it can seem in doubtful taste.

Portato

Not the same as **Portamento**, at least according to some authorities, who use the term to describe a style that is halfway between *legato* and *staccato*—i.e., with the notes not quite smoothly joined.

113

Position

The place of the left hand on the finger-board of a stringed instrument, 'higher' or 'lower' (various positions) according to pitch. Also the place of the slide in trombone playing, where there are seven positions in all.

Postlude

The opposite of a **Prelude**: something played after the main body of a piece, or an organ piece played after a service. Hindemith's *Ludus tonalis* for piano has both a prelude and a postlude of which the latter is a **Retrograde** form of the former.

Precipitato

Rushing and impetuous—e.g., the finale, so marked, of Prokofiev's Seventh Piano Sonata.

Prelude

A solo instrumental piece, perhaps originating in renaissance times with the preludial 'warming-up' of the lute or harpsichord at the start of a suite. Bach likes to pair a prelude with a fugue—e.g., in the '48' Preludes and Fugues for keyboard. Later, the prelude became wholly independent. Chopin, Debussy, Rachmaninov etc, all wrote piano preludes. Debussy's orchestral *'Prélude à l'Après-midi d'un faune'* may originally have been intended to have additional sections.

Presto

Fast. Usually implying a tempo faster than *allegro*. *Prestissimo* means 'very fast'.

Primary Tones
Same as **Natural Notes**.

Programme Music

Instrumental music that seeks to convey a meaning that is literary or visual. There are abundant examples in the keyboard pieces of French composers from Couperin and Rameau to Debussy, Ravel and Messiaen. Liszt's symphonic poems are programmatic, as are those of Richard Strauss, whose *Symphonia Domestica* (1903), for example, has quite a detailed programme. Programme music is today somewhat out of fashion as a compositional method, even Beethoven's 'battle symphony', *Wellingtons Sieg*, having been strongly criticised for its alleged naïveté. Malcolm Arnold's overture *Tam O'Shanter* is, however, a colourful and effective modern example.

Progression
A sequence of chords, two or more.

Psalm
Sacred song or hymn, as in the Bible. Musical settings of the Psalms have been a feature of Jewish and Christian religious services from the earliest times.

Quadrille

French square dance of Napoleonic times, in duple time (2/4 or 6/8), performed by two or four couples, the music being a kind of medley.

Quadrivium

In medieval higher education, the group of four subjects including arithmetic, geometry, music and astronomy. The placing among sciences of what we regard as a fine art tells us something of the medieval approach to music.

Quadruplet

A group of four notes, to be played in the time usually taken by three of the same nominal value.

Quadruple Times

Four beats in a bar—e.g., simple quadruple 4/8, 4/4, 4/2, compound quadruple 12/8, 12/4.

Quartal Harmony

Harmonic system based on fourths, to some extent characteristic of Hindemith's music.

Quarter Note

The crotchet, written ♩♩

Quarter Tone

Half a semitone. Though theoretically perfectly feasible, in practice this interval is little used in western music and indeed is not always available—e.g., on keyboard instruments (though quarter-tone pianos have been made). Around the beginning of the 20th century, a few composers, notably Carrillo and Ives, began to employ quarter tones in their music, with an appropriate notation. It will be understood that stave notation becomes increasingly difficult with sixth tones and even smaller intervals. The Mexican composer Julián Carrillo (1875–1965), perhaps the outstanding pioneer figure in microtonal music, used instead a numerical notation for music involving sixteenth tones. Few of the major figures among 20th-century composers have used quarter tones or indeed other microtones, though Bartók does so, briefly and to some effect, in his First Violin Concerto and Sixth String Quartet.

Quartet

A work for four instruments, commonly in four movements and in sonata form. The string quartet of two violins, viola and cello has from Haydn's time been the chamber-music equivalent of the symphony. (See also **Chamber Music**). Or, a vocal quartet, usually consisting of soprano, alto, tenor and bass.

Quasi

As if, almost—e.g., *quasi da lontano*, as if from afar, *quasi niente*, almost nothing (just audible).

Quaver

The eighth note, written ♪ ♫

Quickstep

A fast **Foxtrot**. The name derives from the parlance of marching (the quick march) but the dance really has nothing in common with military march style.

Quintet

A work for five instruments, commonly in four movements and in sonata form. A string quintet may have two violins, two violas and cello or (as with Schubert's in C major) two violins, viola and two cellos. (The double bass is something of a rarity in chamber music, but features in Schubert's 'Trout' Quintet for piano, violin, viola, cello and double bass.) Wind quintets (flute, oboe, clarinet, bassoon and horn) are not uncommon—e.g., Schoenberg's. A vocal quintet, say in madrigal music, may consist of two sopranos, alto, tenor and bass.

Quintuplet

Quintuplet
A group of five notes, to be played in the time usually taken by three, or four, of the same nominal value.

Quintuple Time
Nominally, five beats in a bar—e.g., simple quintuple 5/8, 5/4, 5/2, compound quintuple 15/8. In practice more like a bar of two irregular beats, thus the 5/4 second movement of Tchaikovsky's Sixth Symphony is really in 2+3/4 time, while Holst's *Mars* has 3+2/4. Uncommon in western art music before the 19th century—though there is an example in the mad scene of Handel's *Orlando* (1732)—but quite frequently met with in folk music—e.g., that of Russia.

Quodlibet
Compilation of existing tunes, either in succession as a medley or polyphonically as in the final variation of Bach's 'Goldberg' Variations for harpsichord. Literally, an 'as-you-please' piece of music.

R

Raga

A characteristic melody type (of which there are many) of Indian music. Each *raga* is of a distinct character, but serves only as the basis for instrumental improvisation, rather than pre-existing as a completed work. There is therefore no notated score as in western music. *Ragas* may be for morning or evening use etc, according to the style. A melody is accompanied by a drone bass and there is no key change (modulation); the instruments might be a *sitar* (a plucked stringed instrument) and a *tabla* (drum), though there are several others. Finally it may be noted that certain *ragas* were, and probably are still, regarded as possessing magic force, bringing rain, healing diseases etc: this is a modern survival of the ancient belief in the mystical power of music.

Ragtime

An American popular piano style that began before 1900—Scott Joplin's 'Maple Leaf Rag' was published in 1899—and came to its most famous period in the few years immediately preceding World War I. This early jazz form, beginning in black music, was to some extent taken over by white musicians (Irving Berlin's 'Alexander's Ragtime Band', 1911); nevertheless 'Jelly Roll' Morton in New Orleans and 'Fats' Waller in New York remain, with Joplin in St Louis, the great names in early piano ragtime. The style is springy and in syncopated duple time, with right-hand

(Left) 'A Raga of Spring' (Jaipur School, 18th century) shows human figures and perhaps also a divine personage in the centre, together with flora and fauna in an exquisitely tended garden

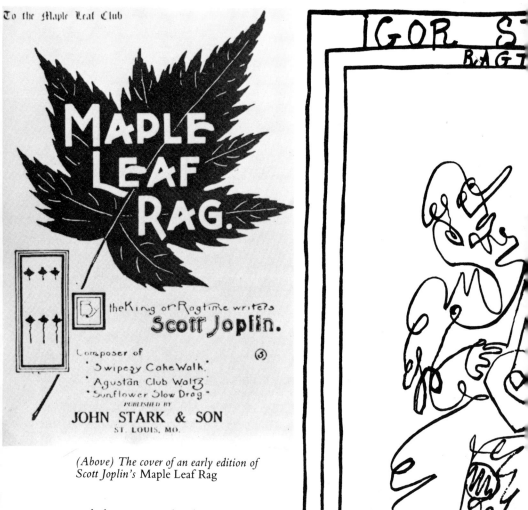

(Above) The cover of an early edition of Scott Joplin's Maple Leaf Rag

melody over a regular chordal bass. The speed is moderate, certainly in the early rags—'it is never right to play ragtime fast', said Joplin. (See also **Jazz**)

Rallentando
Slowing down.

Rank
A set of organ pipes, providing the full pitch range for a single stop.

Recapitulation
That part of a **Sonata-Form** movement, following the development section, in which the material of the exposition is restated with the second subject now in the main (tonic) key.

(Above) Picasso's famous cover illustration for Stravinsky's Ragtime *for eleven instruments (1918)*

Recital

A public performance given by a single performer, perhaps with an accompanist—e.g., a singer, violinist, pianist or organist. If more than two performers are involved, 'concert' is the usual word. It was Liszt who in 1840, as a pianist, brought the term into music from literature.

Recitative

A style of operatic vocal writing in which the rhythms and rise-and-fall of speech are imitated. It emerged seriously, and relatively lyrically, with the earliest Florentine operas at the beginning of the 17th century. But as used by Mozart, for example, recitative has an accompaniment kept to the barest minimum, essentially just keyboard chords, and there is nothing of the lyrical or **Bel canto** style in these rapidly pattering conversational exchanges. The absence of melodic structure (or interest) as such is characteristic of this most prosaic of musical styles. Yet there are expressive recitative-like elements in Wagner's operatic writing, and Debussy's also; and the *Sprechstimme* (see **Speech-song**) of Schoenberg again owes much to recitative. The driest kind of recitative in Italian opera is called appropriately *recitativo secco*. Where the accompaniment is fuller and more sustained the terms *recitativo stromentato* or *recitativo accompagnato* may be employed.

Recte et retro

A **Canon** *per recte et retro* is one in which the following voice or instrumental part has the leader's melody in retrograde (backwards) motion. (See also **Cancrizans**)

Reduction

An arrangement of an ensemble or orchestral piece for a smaller number of instruments, commonly a piano reduction of an orchestral part, such as is printed in the soloist's copy of a concerto.

Reed

Thin piece of cane or metal. That part of a wind instrument (including some organ

Reel

stops) which is made to vibrate and so set the air column vibrating inside the instrument or pipe.

Reel

Lively dance, mainly but not exclusively Scottish and Irish, in duple or quadruple time. The 'Highland Fling' is a vigorous example. So is 'Sir Roger de Coverley' in England and the similar American 'Virginia Reel'.

Refrain

A phrase of words and music that returns at intervals in a song—e.g., at the end of each stanza. Same as a **Burden**.

Reggae

Popular music of Jamaican origin which reached a wider audience in the early 1970s. It blends elements of native folk music and rock music and features strong bass lines and a 'between beat' type of percussion with guitar. Bob Marley, the singer and guitarist, is perhaps the best-known reggae musician. The reggae style is closely associated with the Rastafarian religious movement whose followers believe in the divinity of the late Ethiopian emperor Hailé Selassié.

Register

A part of the compass of a voice or instrument—e.g., the chest register of a voice. 'To register' in organ music is to choose the stops—i.e., a kind of 'instrumentation' of the score. This must be left to some extent to the player since hardly any two organs are identical in specification—and even if they are, registration may well be affected by the acoustics of the building in which an instrument is played.

(Top left) A Scottish reel in 1816. It would be unusual today for the piper to be seated. Evidently the dance was learned young, to judge from the diminutive figures standing thoughtfully in the right foreground.

(Bottom left) Bob Marley at the Sunsplash Festival, Montego Bay, Jamaica, 1979

Réjouissance

A light, playful instrumental piece in baroque music. There is an example in Bach's Fourth Orchestral Suite.

Relative Major and Minor

The relative key is that which shares the same key signature. C major and A minor have this relationship one to another; so do A major and F sharp minor, E flat major and C minor etc. (See also **Circle of Fifths, Key Relationship**)

Relative Pitch

The pitch of a note (tone) relative to another—e.g., a minor 3rd above or a major 2nd below. The ability to recognise such **Intervals** is vastly more important than the possession of **Absolute Pitch**, particularly now that concert pitch itself may vary according to the performers' discretion, at least in some older music.

Renaissance Music

Music between about 1400–1600, preceded by medieval times and followed by the baroque. The renaissance was a wind of change, bringing to music—something of a science to the medieval mind—a new simplicity, a greater humanity and topicality. The Italian **Caccie** (actually of the 14th century) embody this new spirit, as does Italian painting of the period. Chaucer's writing too shows that this mood spread quickly across Europe, where indeed the eclectic humanism of Shakespeare was to represent it at its highest peak of achievement.

The musical achievements of the renaissance include the discovery of a direct and narrative style, with more purposeful harmonic progression than hitherto, indeed the growth of a sense of proportion, of phrase and cadence. All these qualities are exemplified in the music of Josquin des Prés (about 1450–1521), 'the master of the notes' as Martin Luther called him. As for instrumental music, this, with its own forms, really came into independent being only in the 16th century. Finally, it is with the

(Above) 'Wedding at Cana' by the Renaissance painter Veronese—a rich tableau complete with very un-Biblical viols and hounds

renaissance that great individual names appear for the first time in music.

Repeat

The repetition of a section of music is indicated by signs at its beginning and end. If the first sign does not appear, the repeat section is from the beginning of the piece.

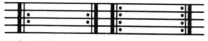

(Above) Repeat signs

Reprise

A repetition or **Recapitulation** in a piece of music of earlier material, though not necessarily in a sonata-form movement.

Requiem

In the Roman Catholic liturgy, the *Missa pro defunctis* or Mass for the Dead, evidently related to the **Mass** though with several changes—e.g., the omission of the *Gloria* and *Credo* and the use of the *Requiem aeternam* and *Dies irae* texts. There are many musical settings of the Requiem text from the 15th century onwards, some elaborate. Among these are the Requiems of Mozart, Berlioz, Verdi and Fauré—this latter omitting the *Dies irae*. The German Requiem by

Brahms uses a non-Catholic German scriptural text. That of Delius has a semi-secular text compiled by the composer, whose beliefs were not orthodox: 'it is not a religious work', he declared. Britten's *War Requiem* intersperses Wilfred Owen's English poems with the Latin liturgical text.

Resolution
The following of dissonance by an appropriate consonance. In practice the latter is usually a **Triad**, though a milder dissonance has the same effect.

Resonance
The transmission of vibrations sympathetically from one body to another. For example, if a low C is struck on the piano, with all the dampers raised, other Cs above it will sound, as will indeed other strings corresponding to the **Harmonics** though in varying amplitude. This accounts for the tonal difference in even a single note, according to whether the right pedal is depressed or not. There is also an effect of 'general resonance', not only from the body of a violin, soundboard of a piano etc, but also from a hall in which music is played.

Responses
In a Christian church service, congregational or choral 'replies' to phrases sung by the priest—e.g., in the versicles.

Rest
The relative values of periods of silence, corresponding to note values, are indicated by symbols. (See also **Note Values, Dot**)

Rests (Above, left to right):
semibreve/whole note, minim/half note,
crotchet/quarter note, quaver/eighth note,
semiquaver/sixteenth note,
demisemiquaver/thirty-second note

Restez
In string music, an instruction not to change **Position** on the fingerboard.

Resultant Tone
A 'third sound' (pitch) resulting from two notes of different pitch together. Also called a 'combination tone'. There are in fact several of these, though in musical practice they may be ignored as being very faint. Resultant tones are divided into two classes, 'differential tones' and 'summation tones' according to the way in which they occur.

Retrograde
'Backwards' motion, the same as **Cancrizans**.

Rhapsody
Nominally an epic poem—e.g., of ancient Greece. The word now implies a dramatically powerful and perhaps structurally free instrumental composition, usually for a solo performer—e.g., those for piano by Liszt and Brahms—though Brahms's *Alto Rhapsody* for voice and orchestra and Gershwin's *Rhapsody in Blue* for piano and orchestra are exceptions.

Rhythm
Literally, the 'flow' of music—that part of music concerned with temporal duration and with accent in its 'shaping' and patterning capacity. Rhythm is concerned with the 'time' side of music in the sense that melody concerns pitch, and is thus fundamental indeed. (See also **Metre, Beat, Bar**)

Rhythmic Modes
Rhythmic patterns in medieval music from about the late 12th century. There were six of these, derived from the metric

feet of poetry—e.g., the long-short alternation of the trochee that became a minim, crotchet (half note, quarter note) pattern in 3/4 time.

Ribs
The sides of stringed instruments—e.g., of the violin family.

Ricercar
A polyphonic and (usually) instrumental composition of the renaissance and baroque periods, with elaborate imitative technique, akin to that of the vocal motet. The six-part *ricercare* (an alternative spelling) in Bach's *Musical Offering* is a celebrated late example. Literally, something 'carefully worked', even *recherché*.

Rigaudon
Lively 17th-century French dance from Provence in duple or quadruple time, found in Lully, Bach etc and more recently in Ravel's *Le Tombeau de Couperin*. Called 'rigadoon' by Purcell.

Ripieno
Literally, 'full'. The larger body of players in a baroque concerted work such as a *concerto grosso*, the smaller group being the *concertino*.

Ritardando
'Holding back'—i.e., slowing down—much the same as *rallentando*. Often abbreviated *ritard* or *rit*. See also **Ritenuto**.

Ritenuto
Held back—i.e., slower. Often abbreviated *rit*.

Ritornello
A passage that returns, often more than once—e.g., the main theme in a rondoform movement. (But the term is used pretty loosely.)

(Below) Watteau's painting 'The Scale of Love' depicts an elegant scene in some idealised rococo garden.

Rococo

The elegantly ornate style of the 18th century immediately before the classical period, also called **Galant** style. Some scholars characterise it as essentially frivolous, lacking the substance and seriousness of the baroque or indeed of classicism as exemplified in, say, the mature Mozart. Yet there are of course ornamental, even 'pretty' features in Mozart, and for that matter in Bach also, that may fairly be regarded as rococo in style.

(Below) The wilder aspects of romanticism are caricatured in this 'Liszt' montage published in La vie parisienne *in 1886.*

Romance

A song or instrumental piece of tender or passionate character—e.g., the slow movement of Mozart's D minor Piano Concerto K.466, or Schumann's F sharp major *Romanze*, Op 28, for piano. (*Romanze* is the German word.)

Romanticism

A 19th-century movement in music, characterised by a greater element than hitherto of deliberate self-expression on the part of composers who set out to explore the full range of the human spirit. Walter Pater defined romanticism as 'the addition of strangeness to beauty', while among musicians Schumann said that he would not like 'to be understood by everybody' and Berlioz made a similar remark. Love, heroism and death all inspired the romantics: literature and music came close together in Schubert's song cycles, Berlioz's symphonies, Liszt's symphonies and symphonic poems, Wagner's music dramas (operas) and, at the end of the era, such works as Strauss's *Ein Heldenleben*, Mahler's Eighth Symphony and Schoenberg's *Erwartung*. Even where literature is not directly involved, such music as Mendelssohn's Violin Concerto, Schumann's piano sonatas and Chopin's nocturnes, as well as the symphonies of Brahms and Tchaikovsky, are imbued with qualities of feeling that are above all personal to their composers. At the turn of the century, both Debussy's impressionism and Schoenberg's expressionism are easily be related to the romantic movement. The **Nationalism** of Russian and other the same words. Later, an instrumental form in 17th-century music—e.g., Couperin's—that is the same as the more modern **Rondo**.

Rondo

A musical form in which a main theme, heard at the outset, returns at intervals, usually still in the tonic key, and finally closes the piece. In fact rondo form is an extension of ternary form (A, B, A) into something like A, B, A, C, A, D, A. Varieties exist—e.g., replacing D in the previous example by B and so creating a structure sometimes called 'sonata rondo'. Rondo form is a feature of the Italian baroque solo concerto—e.g., Vivaldi—and became common in classical finales such as Beethoven's.

Root

The harmonic bass (generating note, principal note) of a **Triad**, or of some other chord such as a dominant seventh derived from a triad by the addition of notes, in its original position—i.e., a triad formed by adding the 3rd and 5th above to a degree (note) of a scale. The root of the C major triad (C, E, G) is thus C, even when the chord is placed in **Inversion**.

Rota

A **Round**.

Roulade

A run of notes, as in a highly ornamented vocal passage—much the same as **Divisions**.

Round

A type of **Canon** at the unison or octave in which each voice returns to the start, without pause, on completing the tune. Usually a round is made to end by each voice having, say, three statements only of the tune. The voices thus both begin and end the round in turn. Usually there are three voices or more. (See also **Catch**)

Round Dance

A dance in which the dancers move around in a circle.

A 'Schubert Evening' in 1826. The composer is at the piano. In this quietly romantic circle, those present include the dramatist Grillparzer, the painter Moritz von Schwind and the singer Vogl.

composers, in so far as its ideal is the expression of a nation's 'soul', may also be regarded as essentially part of romantic thought. Elgar and Rachmaninov are normally thought of as romantics, ending the era; while Stravinsky's neoclassical works after 1920 mark a clear move away to other fields.

Rondeau

A medieval song 'form', allotting two musical phrases to various lines in a poetic stanza—e.g., A, B, a, A, a, b, A, B, where the capitals indicate choral lines to

Roundelay
An English term for the French *rondelet*, i.e., *rondeau* in the sense of a simple song.

Rubato
Rhythmic flexibility. Artistically used, it is wholly natural and unobtrusive. Much that is inaccurate has been written, and taught, about *rubato*. There is no need for exact give-and-take, for example, with any *accelerando* being compensated for by a corresponding *rallentando*. Nor is it true that *rubato* is only appropriate in solo pieces, or in 19th-century romantic music. Tempo flexibility—a kind of large-scale *rubato*—is not only a feature of Elgar's recorded conducting of his own music, but occurs also in the much-praised performances of Beethoven's symphonies by Herbert von Karajan, and those of other conductors.

Rumba
Lively Afro-Cuban dance, popular also in jazz. The usual rhythm, in 4/4, has syncopated accents on the 4th and 7th quavers (eighth notes) in a busy quaver accompaniment. The finale of Milhaud's *Scaramouche* is a rumba, though not so-called. (It seems that the original Cuban rumba was rhythmically more complex.)

S

Saeta
Spanish penitential song, sung outdoors during religious street processions—e.g., in Lent.

Saltarello
A very lively Italian dance deriving its name from *saltare*, to leap. In triple time, or 6/8. The finale of Mendelssohn's 'Italian' Symphony is mainly in *saltarello* style.

Samba
Brazilian dance, lively and syncopated in its duple rhythm. The most characteristic music of the famous Rio de Janeiro carnival.

Saraband
Triple-time dance of Latin (perhaps Mexican) origin. The original saraband of the 16th century was fast and even wild. Later a slow and stately form appeared, 'full of state and ancientry', as Shakespeare has it. In the latter style, a standard dance of the baroque instrumental suite—e.g., those of Bach.

Scale
The notes of a key, arranged in order of pitch. (See **Major, Melodic Minor, Harmonic Minor, Chromatic, Pentatonic Scale, Whole-tone Scale, Modes.**)

Scat Singing
A 'hot' jazz singing style of the 1920s with improvised 'nonsense words', adopted by Cab Calloway and Louis Armstrong among others.

(Right) The stately saraband, depicted by a German artist

Scherzando
Playfully.

Scherzo
Literally, a 'joke'. This instrumental piece in fast triple time succeeded the statelier minuet as the standard third movement of a symphony, string quartet or other four-movement sonata-type work. The scherzo was used by Haydn in some of his string quartets and became the norm in the 19th-century symphony

etc. But the 'joke' element has virtually disappeared in certain scherzos. We may think of those of Beethoven's Fifth and Ninth Symphonies—not, however, actually labelled scherzos—and of Mahler's symphonies; while Chopin's four independent piano scherzos are, with the exception of the last, more dramatic than playful, proceeding also at such a brisk pace that one really counts whole bars rather than beats. Mendelssohn's scherzos, on the other hand, have a delightful lightness. Like the minuet, a scherzo is usually in **Ternary Form**.

Schottische
19th-century round dance, nothing to do with Scotland despite the name, and similar to the **Polka**. In England it was sometimes called the 'German polka'.

Scordatura
Non-standard tuning of a stringed instrument—e.g., at the start of Saint-Saëns's *Danse macabre*, where the solo violin tunes his E string down to E flat. Bach uses *scordatura* in his Fifth Cello Suite, as does Kodály in his unaccompanied Sonata for the same instrument. The solo violinist in the second movement of Mahler's Fourth Symphony must tune a tone higher so that his timbre may suggest that of a country fiddle. *Scordatura* is uncommon and little liked by players because of its effect on timbre and the difficulty of retuning during the course of the music.

Score
The notated form of a piece of music—i.e., the copy. A full score shows all the parts, whether playing or not; a miniature score has a reduced format and omits temporarily non-playing instruments; a vocal score has voice parts with orchestra reduced for performance on the piano—e.g., in study or rehearsal. 'Scoring' is another word for orchestration.

Second
The interval between two notes two letter names apart, inclusive—e.g., C–D. This is a major second. A diminution

by a semitone—e.g., C–D flat or C sharp–D—gives a minor second, while C–D sharp and C flat–D are augmented seconds.

Second Subject
The second theme (or group of themes sharing the same key) of a sonata-form movement, appearing in the **Exposition** in a related key and later in the recapitulation in the main (tonic) key. (See also **Key Relationship**)

Secondary Seventh
A chord consisting of a note, plus its 3rd, 5th and 7th, formed on any degree of the scale other than the dominant—i.e., not the dominant seventh chord. Some would perhaps also exclude the diminished seventh chord occurring on the leading note of the minor scale.

Seguidilla
Southern Spanish dance, or dance song, in quick triple time. There is an attractive piano '*Seguidilla*' in F sharp major by Albéniz.

Semibreve
The whole note, written **o**

Semichorus
Small section of a choral body, literally a half-chorus but not necessarily so in practice.

Semiquaver
The sixteenth note, written ♪ 𝄾

Semitone
The half-tone—e.g., C–D flat.

Semplice
Simply.

Sempre
Always.

Senza
Without.

Septet

A work for seven instruments, commonly in four movements and in sonata form. Beethoven's Septet in E flat major, Op 20, is for clarinet, horn, bassoon, violin, viola, cello and double bass.

Septuplet

A group of seven notes to be played in the time usually taken by four or six of the same nominal value.

The seguidilla, *danced to the sound of a guitar in southern Spain*

Sequence

A series of more or less exact repetitions of a figure at different pitches. Alternatively, a section of music originally added to the *alleluia* in early Church plainchant that eventually developed independent life in the 12th century and led to such elaborate examples as the *Dies irae* and *Stabat mater*.

Serenade

An 'evening piece', its character usually agreeable and light, vocal—e.g., Schubert's *Ständchen*—or instrumental. The latter type is usually in several movements—e.g., those by Mozart, Tchaikovsky and Elgar. Britten's vocal *Serenade* (1943) is a song cycle on poems whose subject is evening.

Serial music

Music in which the kind of order which we call 'key' is replaced by a series of intervals chosen by the composer, and perhaps also durational values, dynamic levels etc, which themselves form the basic 'method' according to which the composition takes place. The **Twelve-note Music** of Schoenberg is the prototype, emerging after much thought in the 1920s from the free atonality of such works as *Pierrot Lunaire* (1912). Later composers using serial techniques to a greater or lesser extent include Messiaen (in his piano study called *Modes de valeurs et d'intensités*, 1949), Boulez (*Le Marteau sans Maître*, 1955) and Stockhausen (*Zeitmasse*, 1956). The 'intervallic' aspects of late Stravinsky are serial also. In America, Milton Babbitt has used serial technique extensively, Copland rarely but interestingly as in his piano Variations written as early as 1930.

Service

The order of events in the Christian liturgy, though the term is commonly reserved for the Communion, Morning and Evening Prayer of the Anglican Church. A piece of music called a service consists of settings of the **Canticles**, creed etc. The service settings of Byrd, Purcell and Wesley are notable examples from their respective periods.

Seventh

The interval between two notes seven letter names apart, inclusive—e.g., C–B. This is a major seventh. A diminution by a semitone—e.g., C–B flat, C sharp–B—gives a minor seventh, while C sharp–B flat is a diminished seventh.

Sextet

A work for six instruments, commonly in four movements and in sonata form—e.g., Brahms's two works, Opp 18 and 36, for two violins, two violas and two cellos.

Sextolet

A group of six notes to be played in the time usually taken by four of the same nominal value.

Sforzando

Accented, emphasised. Usually abbreviated *sf*.

Shake

Same as a **Trill**.

Shanty

A sailors' work song, formerly used to coordinate group movements—e.g., hauling on ropes. The term derives from the French *chanté*, sung.

Sharp

The sign indicating the raising of a note by a semitone without changing its letter name or its position on the stave. As an adjective, 'sharp' may describe singing or playing out of tune, above correct pitch. (See **Accidental** for illustration)

Shift

Change of **Position** on a stringed instrument.

Siciliano

Dance of Sicilan origin, in 6/8 or 12/8 time, gently flowing and pastoral in character. There is a famous example by Fauré, originally for cello with piano but also often played on the flute. Also spelt *siciliana* and *sicilienne*.

Sight-reading

Performing music while reading it for the first time. Orchestral players and choral singers must do this as a matter of course; but the complex nature of keyboard music makes such reading harder for a pianist or organist, who in addition cannot look at both the score and the keyboard.

Similar Motion

Movement of two parts in the same direction. If the interval between them does not change, this is also called **Parallel Motion**.

Simile

A direction to continue playing in the same way—e.g., *staccato*—with the same kind of bowing etc.

Simple Time

A time (i.e., pattern of beats) in which the beat is a plain (undotted) note—e.g., 2/4, 3/8.

Sinfonia

The Italian word for symphony. It was used in baroque times for the overture to an opera or other extended vocal work. Bach also used the term *sinfonia* (it is not clear why) for his three-part keyboard inventions.

Sinfonia Concertante

See **Concertante**.

Sinfonietta

A short symphony, perhaps also using a small orchestra.

Singspiel

German opera, with German text, usually light and even comic in style. In 1743 an English ballad opera called *The Devil to Pay* was successfully performed with German words in Berlin, and later Johann Adam Hiller (1728–1804) took up the style, so that he is sometimes called the 'father of the *Singspiel*'. Mozart called his *Die Entführung aus dem Serail* (1782) a *Singspiel*, and his *Zauberflöte* too, despite its more serious story, has something of the *Singspiel* about it. Later *Singspiel* (such as Wranitżky's *Oberon*, 1790, and Hoffmann's *Undine*, 1816) paved the way to 19th-century romantic German opera, notably Weber. It should also not be forgotten that Schubert wrote five *Singspiele*, including *Die Zwillingsbrüder* (1820).

Six-four Chord

The second inversion of a triad—e.g., G–C–E or G–C–E flat. Often followed by the dominant chord (in this case, on G) and then the tonic in a perfect cadence (full close). It is so-called because of the intervals above the bass note, a 4th and 6th.

Sixteenth Note

The semiquaver, written ♪

Sixth

The interval between two notes six letter names apart, inclusive—e.g., C–A. This is a major sixth. A diminution by a semitone—e.g., C–A flat, C sharp–A—gives a minor sixth, while C–A sharp is an augmented sixth.

Slancio

'Dash', impetuosity, *élan*.

Slentando

Slowing down, relaxing.

Slide

The string **Portamento**, or the moving part of the trombone tubing.

Slur

Curved line, placed over two or more notes, indicating *legato*—i.e., smooth playing.

Smorzando

Dying away.

Solfège

A system of vocal exercises, sung to a vowel or the tonic sol-fa syllables, used for training in sight-reading, perhaps especially in France. More broadly, instruction in the general rudiments of music.

Solmisation

A system of designating the notes of a diatonic scale by syllables—e.g., *do, re, mi, fa, sol* (or *soh*), *la, ti*, similar to those introduced with the **Hexachord** in the 11th century.

Solo

A passage for a single performer, either wholly alone or clearly standing out over some form of accompaniment.

Sonata

An instrumental work, normally in three or four movements, for one or two performers. The first movement is commonly in **Sonata Form** and is followed by an expressive slow movement, an (optional) minuet or scherzo, and a brisk finale. The term comes from the Italian *suonare*, to play. The classical sonata emerged in the 18th century and matured with the Viennese masters from Haydn to Schubert. Like its orchestral counterpart, the symphony, it has remained valid both for the 19th-century romantics and the composers of today—though Boulez, for example, has moved a long way indeed from the structure outlined above. Liszt's Piano Sonata in B minor is in one long movement; the one-movement sonatas for harpsichord by Domenico Scarlatti were originally called *essercizi*, studies. (See also **Sonata Form, Camera, Chiesa**)

Sonata Form

The form commonly employed for the first movement of a sonata and indeed of other works not so called—trios, quartets etc—as well as concertos and symphonies, which are structurally similar. Two contrasting themes, in two related key areas, are announced in the exposition, which may be repeated; then comes a development section based on this material, perhaps treated motivically with modulating passages, followed by a recapitulation which generally resembles the exposition though without the key change between the first and second themes (properly called 'subjects'). The second-subject section may have more than one theme, but these will share the same key. An introduction may open a sonata-form movement, and a coda may end it. (See also **Exposition, Development, Recapitulation, Introduction, Coda**)

Sonatina

A short sonata, perhaps not too demanding technically.

Song

A piece of music for a solo voice, commonly with accompaniment but not necessarily so. The form is known in all periods, from ancient Greek music onwards, and in all cultures. The medieval **Troubadour, Trouvère** and **Minnesinger** songs, together with other styles including that of church singing, led to the **Meistersinger** period in the 16th century and, slightly later in England, the *ayre* as exemplified in the lute songs of Dowland, whose first such collection appeared in 1597. Dowland had a distinguished English successor in Purcell (1659–95).

The operatic arias of the 17th and 18th centuries are of course also songs, though in a wider dramatic context and without the intimate quality associated with song generally. So are the sacred songs—e.g., of a Bach cantata. But it was the area of folk song that proved a more fruitful source for the German *Lied*, Russian song style and French *mélodie* of the 19th century. The personal nature of song appealed greatly to the romantic composers, who perhaps above all enriched this repertory. The 20th century has seen a rich variety also in song-writing, from traditionalists such as Rachmaninov in Russia and Quilter in England to advanced composers from Ives *via* Stravinsky and Webern to Boulez and

Maxwell Davies. Many attractive and lasting 20th-century songs have come also from the stylistic middle ground: and to this repertory there have been major contributions from Debussy, Poulenc, Shostakovich and Britten. (See also **Lied**)

Song Cycle

A series of songs, usually unified by a literary theme or, at least, some overall mood—e.g., Schubert's 'Die schöne Müllerin', which tells a clear story, or Fauré's 'La bonne chanson' to Verlaine's gently romantic poems.

Song Form

Another name for ternary (A, B, A) form, used in 18th-century arias, both operatic and in such works as Bach's cantatas. But it should be noted that the **Strophic Song** form is both older and more usual.

Soprano

The high-range female voice, with a compass of nearly two octaves above middle C. A coloratura soprano has a high, light and brilliant voice, while lyric and dramatic sopranos offer the other qualities implied by these names.

Sordino

Mute. Hence con sordino and senza sordino are instructions respectively to put on and to take off the **Mute**—e.g., of a stringed or wind instrument.

Sostenuto

Sustained tone. In Brahms's music, it often means also a slackening of pace.

Soundboard

The wooden surface over which the strings of a piano are stretched, and which vibrates sympathetically with them.

Sound Hole

An opening cut for acoustical reasons in the body of a stringed instrument—e.g., the so-called 'F holes' of a violin, of which there are two, one on each side of the bridge.

Sound Post

A small piece of wood fixed inside a violin or other bowed stringed instrument, to support the 'table'—i.e., the front part of the body—and also to convey vibrations.

Spacing

The arrangement of the notes of a chord, close or open as the case may be.

Speech-song

The Sprechstimme of Schoenberg's Pierrot Lunaire and some other works—e.g., Henze's El Cimarrón (1970). (See also **Declamation**)

Spiccato

A bowing style involving light, detached notes 'bounced' on the string. Also called saltando and sautillé.

Spirito

Spirit, wit, vitality.

Spiritual

Black religious song style of America, though arguably strongly influenced by the similar white sacred music that also exists, widely known through publication after the 1868 collection called Slave Songs of the United States, edited by W. F. Allen. Titles such as 'Deep River', 'Steal away to Jesus' etc, are familiar and characteristic. The singing of the late Paul Robeson is closely associated with this repertory.

Sprechstimme
See **Speech-song**

Square Dance

A dance in which those taking part form a rectangle, rather than the circle of a 'round dance'.

Staccato

Short, detached notes: the opposite of legato playing. Indicated by a dot over or below the note. The superlative is staccatissimo. A half-staccato (mezzo staccato) may be indicated by a slur over or under the dots.

The soprano Maria Callas sings Tosca, *one of her most famous roles, with Tito Gobbi as Scarpia.*

Stave
The five horizontal lines upon and between which the notes are placed in notated music.

Steel Band
A Caribbean ensemble, whose traditional instruments are oil drums with their heads worked in such a way that they will produce different notes. The sound is surprisingly well-tuned and delicate.

Stomp
In jazz, a kind of vigorous march—e.g., 'King Porter Stomp', 'Chattanooga' etc.

Stop
On the organ or harpsichord, a device for bringing in a particular rank of pipes, muffled string tone etc. Or the actual rank of pipes etc.

Stopping
In string playing, pressing a finger on to a string to fix its vibrating length and so determine the note it will produce. On the horn, stopping means muting the

rhythm—i.e., *accelerando*—as in the closing passages of Chopin's C sharp minor Scherzo for piano.

Strophic Song

A song in which the music is repeated, exactly or with a degree of variation, with each stanza of the poetic text. Hymns are usually strophic, and so are many art songs of the 19th century—e.g., those by Schubert. (But his '*Erlkönig*', for example, is through-composed, with fresh music for each stanza.)

Study

Same as **Etude**.

Style

A hard word to define. It is the manner, the whole complex of generally identifiable and recognisable features, that gives distinct character to music, whether it be a single piece or the whole *oeuvre* of a composer or performer. We may talk, for example, of Stravinsky's style, or perhaps Stravinsky's later style, or even, more generally, of a twentieth-century style.

Some would argue that style and content are really inseparable, the 'manner' and 'matter' of art being merely two ways of looking at it. At a simplistic level, a musician's style may be like his fingerprints or at any rate his handwriting: something which will develop naturally (it cannot be forced) like a personality, but then is indissolubly his own. Style affects not only notes, but also rhythm, form, instrumentation etc. For example, it may well be that a single chord of C major, scored for orchestra by Schumann, Sibelius and Stravinsky, would in each case reveal the artist's identity to an experienced ear.

Subdominant

The fourth note of the major or minor scale—e.g., F in C major or minor.

Subject

Theme—e.g., that of a fugue, or the first and second subjects of a movement in sonata form.

tone (and also perhaps changing the pitch) by putting the hand into the bell.

Strathspey

A slow Scottish dance in quadruple time, the slow counterpart of the reel, featuring the short-long rhythm (with the short note accented) called the 'Scotch snap'.

Strepitoso

Noisy.

Stretto

Literally, 'drawn together' (see **Fugue**). Also occasionally a 'tightening-up' of

Subito
Suddenly, at once.

Submediant
The sixth note of the major or minor scale—e.g., A in C major, A flat in C minor. So-called because it is half-way between the tonic and its subdominant a fifth below.

Suite
A set of instrumental pieces grouped together, more loosely than the movements of a sonata. In the 16th century two or more dance movements were sometimes published as a group of this kind; and with the work of Johann Jacob Froberger (1616–67) the baroque suite took shape, with three movements. These were the allemande, courante and saraband. By the time of Bach (1685–1750) the common layout was as follows: allemande, courante, saraband, . . . gigue, with the space before the final gigue occupied by one or more other dances—e.g., a minuet, gavotte, bourrée etc. The same key was used throughout. (The French *ordre*—e.g., in Couperin, is freer.)

In classical times, the dance suite rather ceased to interest composers, though such forms as the divertimento and cassation followed its tradition. But in the 19th century the idea of grouping pieces other than in sonata-form works became once more attractive. Suites from ballet and from dramatic incidental music reached the concert hall (Tchaikovsky's *Nutcracker* and Bizet's *L'Arlésienne*, for example) and there are also wholly independent suites such as Rimsky-Korsakov's *Scheherazade* and Holst's *Planets*.

Sul ponticello
Literally, 'on the bridge': in fact it means bowing—e.g., on a violin—close to the bridge and so producing a special, rather harsh tonal quality.

Sul tasto
Bowing over the fingerboard or near it—e.g., on a violin—for a veiled tonal quality.

Supertonic
The second note of the major or minor scale—e.g., D in C major or minor.

Suspension
A note or notes held over from one chord into the next, creating a dissonance that is usually resolved by a downward step.

Swing
A development of jazz dating from the few years of the 1930s preceding World War II, with big bands playing elaborate—and of course written-down—arrangements in a sophisticated and carefully presented way. These bands were led by mainly white musicians such as Benny Goodman, Artie Shaw, Harry James, and Jimmy and Tommy Dorsey. Swing has been called 'the beat that lies at the center of jazz'. Though this definition is not especially illuminating, it is true that despite the elaborate big-band orchestration this music retained at its best a genuine improvisatory jazz quality, notably in the work of the Count Basie Band. The band of Jimmie Lunceford has been called the ultimate type of 'show band' of the swing era. As for Duke Ellington, it has been argued that while his arranged passages were in swing style, every solo was authentic jazz. Probably the term 'swing' has been too variously used for any firm definition to be possible. The alto saxophonist Benny Carter called it simply 'the feeling you put into the performance'. In this sense it is what the English call 'dash', the French *élan*—indeed the same as the German word *Schwung* that existed long before jazz itself.

Sword Dance
A folk dance for men, in which the dancers (at least in England) carry imitation swords, each man holding the hilt of his own and the tip of his neighbour's. A dancer may jump over or pass under his neighbour's sword in an elaborate group movement. The Scottish sword dance is

(Right) The Jimmie Lunceford Orchestra plays swing, c. 1934.

different, the swords being laid on the ground to define the area for the dancer's steps: it is to **Strathspey** music.

Symphonic Poem

A programmatic orchestral work in one movement, with a literary or pictorial theme that may be merely stated in the title—e.g., Tchaikovsky's *Hamlet*, actually called an Overture-Fantasy—or may be more fully laid out—e.g., Richard Strauss's *Also sprach Zarathustra*. The term 'Symphonic Poem', in German *Symphonische Dichtung*, was first used in 1854 in connection with Liszt's *Tasso*, one of a series of thirteen such compositions that Liszt wrote between 1848–82. Indeed it is Liszt who is usually thought of as the 'father of the symphonic poem',

though such works as Beethoven's overtures 'Egmont' and 'Coriolan' are progenitors of the form. The symphonic poem belongs very much to the romantic movement of the 19th century; nevertheless it survives in the 20th not only with Richard Strauss but also with Scriabin, Rachmaninov, Elgar and Sibelius.

Symphony

Literally, 'sounds together'. An extended orchestral work, usually in four movements and in sonata form—i.e., an orchestral 'sonata' consisting of a substantial first movement, slow movement, minuet or scherzo and finale. From the late 18th century onwards, the symphony has been the most imposing of instrumental forms both in terms of

length and of the size of instrumental force used.

The word *sinfonia* occurs from the 17th century onwards and may refer to an operatic or other overture, or an instrumental interlude in a vocal work such as the 'Pastoral Symphony' in Handel's *Messiah*. The Italian operatic overture of Alessandro Scarlatti and others had three sections, fast-slow-fast. These overtures could be performed independently, and other works with this structure also came into being. As the three sections or movements grew in substance, it was easy to borrow the already existing forms of the baroque concerto such as song-like slow movements emphasising melody, rondos and sets of variations, while brisk finales (such as those of Bach's concertos) became the norm. The late 18th-century classical symphony was prepared by a number of musicians, among them Johann Stamitz and C. P. E. Bach. Stamitz, with his famous Mannheim orchestra, introduced the still-new clarinets to the standard ensemble of wind and strings and made famous a dramatic *crescendo* effect that was only possible with well-disciplined players. C. P. E. Bach, a progressive exponent of the highly expressive *Sturm und Drang* (storm and stress) school in music, opened doors for both Haydn and Mozart, as they later acknowledged, in the realm of expressive instrumental writing.

The classical symphony up to Beethoven's time was perhaps twenty minutes in length. Beethoven doubled this as necessary—e.g., in his Third Symphony) and introduced trombones into symphonic writing. He also made two innovations: the use of a literary programme (requiring five movements) in his 'Pastoral' Symphony and the use of voices, and therefore also an explicit literary text, in the finale of his Ninth. During the romantic period which followed, both of these were followed up—e.g., by Berlioz, whose *Simphonie Fantastique* (1830) is programmatic and whose 'symphonie dramatique' *Roméo et Juliette* employs voices. The two prog-

rammatic symphonies of Liszt and even Wagner's music dramas (operas) also represent developments of the 'poetic' aspect of Beethoven's symphonic works. So perhaps, to some extent, do Dvořák's, Franck's and Tchaikovsky's symphonies. On the other hand, Mendelssohn, Schumann and Brahms seem to remain closer to the classical ideal; much later, so does Sibelius.

No fundamental changes have taken place in symphonic form during the 20th century. Strauss's mature symphonies are programmatic and Mahler's (often with the voice) sometimes so. Britten's *Spring Symphony* is vocal throughout, while Schoenberg and Webern wrote chamber-orchestral symphonies. But the symphonies of Elgar, Rachmaninov, Vaughan Williams, Prokofiev, Shostakovich and even Stravinsky, though powerful and personal, are not innovatory in the technical sense. (Though in his *Symphonies of Wind Instruments* Stravinsky employs the term merely in its oldest sense of 'ensemble music'.) Among American symphonies, those of Charles Ives stand out as landmarks—but here again, not so much for their form as for their harmonic language.

New symphonies are commissioned today from young as well as established composers and receive performances, but their chances of finding a permanent place in the orchestral repertory are slim. New, especially non-tonal, techniques of musical invention seem to accord ill with large-scale instrumental forms. Few musicians would care to name any indisputable symphonic masterpiece of the last thirty years, save for Shostakovich's last works in this form.

Syncopation

Displacement of normal accent, by emphasis on a weak beat rather than a strong, or by an accent falling between the beats. Scott Joplin's piano rag 'The Entertainer' offers a well-known

(Right) 'A Symphony': this elaborate composite painting is by Schubert's friend Moritz von Schwind (1804–71).

Synthesiser

example. (But Joplin does not bother to mark any accents, which in any case are not only dynamic—i.e., of loudness—but also agogic—i.e., of note-length.)

Synthesiser

The electronic apparatus that 'creates' sound according to instructions given by the player *via* one or more keyboards, stops etc. The synthesiser can of course be played like any other instrument, though its sound must emerge through a loudspeaker. What distinguishes it from, say, the electronic organ is the way in which new timbres, hitherto unheard, can be instantly created by the performer, and also the way in which its music can be 'played', soundlessly if need be, directly on to magnetic recording tape. A synthesiser performance—e.g., Debussy piano music by the Japanese Isao Tomita—may be a very elaborate instrumentation built up little by little on multi-track tape. It therefore cannot possibly take place 'live'. (See also **Electronic Instruments, Electronic Music**.)

System

The staves, two or more, used to notate a piece of music—e.g., the four staves required in a string quartet score or the eight staves required for an octet. The system for piano music normally consists of two staves.

Tablature

A notational system of renaissance times, mainly for the lute and keyboard, in which the notes are indicated by figures, letters or in some other way different to that of standard stave notation. It survives today in guitar and ukelele music, showing finger positions for chords by blobs (like note-heads) placed on a lattice of vertical and horizontal lines representing the strings and frets of the instrument.

Tangent

The small metal 'touchers' that strike the

Tablature: an example of this notation from an Italian lute book

(Above) The 'Argentine tango, a cake-walk played adagio', in early 20th-century Paris

strings of a clavichord when the keys are depressed.

Tango

Argentinian dance of the 20th century, with a characteristic, lazy rhythm, not unlike the **Habañera**. There is a well-known piano Tango in D major by Albéniz as well as numerous tangos of lighter music—e.g., 'Jealousy'.

Tarantella

A southern Italian dance in brisk 6/8 time, characterised by a steady flow of quick notes like that of a **Perpetuum mobile**. There is a well-known Tarantella for piano by Chopin, and there are

tarantella-like passages also in the finale of Mendelssohn's 'Italian' Symphony. The name probably derives from that of the town Taranto.

Tedesca

An early name for the **Allemande**. Both terms mean 'German'—i.e., a German dance. Also applied to the **Ländler**, hence Beethoven's *alla tedesca* marking in two G major movements: one in his Piano Sonata in G major, Op 79, and the other in his String Quartet in B flat major, Op 130.

Temperament

A system of tuning. Equal temperament, in use since baroque times, ignores the minute pitch differences existing between certain notes—e.g., C sharp and D flat—in order to restrict the number of pitches within the octave to the twelve notes of the **Chromatic** scale. This makes all of these notes available as a tonic in a total of twenty-four major and minor keys—as illustrated, twice over, in Bach's 'Forty-Eight' Preludes and Fugues. (See also **Enharmonic**)

Tempo

Speed. Commonly indicated by **Metronome** marks, or by such words as *largo, lento, adagio, andante, moderato, allegro, presto* etc, placed at the beginning of a piece or of a section at a new speed. Tempo markings normally need not be adhered to rigidly, however, but treated as a norm around which the speed may fluctuate. Debussy once said that a metronome mark might only indicate the precise speed 'for a single bar'.

Teneramente

Tenderly.

Tenor

The high-range broken male voice, with a compass of about one and a half octaves, perhaps more, above the C in the bass clef. The various kinds of tenor voice are sometimes characterised by the terms 'lyric tenor' or '*Heldentenor*' (with a heroic timbre and vigour). The term 'tenor' is also applied in medieval music to that voice part which sings a *cantus firmus*, in other words the original polyphonic part to which others have been added.

Tenth
The interval between two notes ten letter names apart, inclusive—e.g., C up to the E beyond the octave C. This is a major tenth. A semitone decrease (C–E flat or C sharp–E) gives a minor tenth.

Tenuto
Literally, 'held': a slight pause on a note, or simply a careful *legato* style.

Ternary Form
Three-part form, with an A, B, A structure. One of the commonest of musical forms, it is that, for example, of the minuet, where the so-called 'trio section' provides the contrasting central part of the piece and is followed by a return of the opening music. A slow movement may be in ternary form, for example the 'Romanze' of Mozart's D minor Piano Concerto, K.466, with its strongly contrasting middle section producing a dramatic effect. The same kind of powerful contrasts often occur in the ternary-form nocturnes of Chopin—e.g., those in F major and F sharp major, Op 15.

Tessitura
The general range of an instrumental or vocal part—e.g., lying 'high' or 'low'.

Tetrachord
Not a chord, but a four-note scale or sequence of pitches, such as was used in ancient Greek music as a melodic basis for song or instrumental playing. The outer notes were a perfect fourth apart, but the inner notes could be more freely pitched. Later, in medieval musical theory, the tetrachord could simply be the first four notes of a **Hexachord**.

Theme
A melodic idea of distinct character forming the main material of a piece, or more commonly of a section of a piece. The same as **Subject**. In a ternary-form piece, the first theme will be succeeded by another of contrasting character, normally in a different key; a return to the original theme, which must be recognised, then takes place. A theme must therefore be memorable. This is perhaps even more important in sonata form, where two themes of contrasting nature are followed by a development section in which the listener should be aware of what is being done to the previously stated thematic material. The theme of a set of variations is subjected to alteration and elaboration without, however, losing its identity. There is little difference between theme and **Tune**.

Third
The interval between two notes three letter names apart, inclusive—e.g., C–E. This is a major third. A diminution by a semitone—e.g., C–E flat or C sharp–E—gives a minor third.

Thirty-second Note
The demisemiquaver, written ♪ ♪

Thorough Bass
Same as **Figured Bass**.

Through-composed
A song is said to be through-composed if it has fresh music for each stanza of a poem—i.e., if it is not in **Strophic** form. Schubert's 'Erlkönig' is an example.

Tie
The curved line joining two written notes that in fact represent a single sustained sound. It is used where one single note cannot be written—e.g., when the note extends through a bar line or when it has an irregular length so that no suitable note value exists.

Tierce de Picardie
The tonic major third (really the use of the major chord) replacing the tonic minor at the end of a minor-mode composition. Its use is common, indeed the

Timbre

rule rather than the exception, in baroque music and earlier, perhaps because of a feeling of greater finality or that the minor chord was less consonant. The 'Picardy' name, used from the 18th century, has not been explained.

Timbre
Tone colour. (See also **Harmonics**)

Time
The pattern of beats in a piece of music. Also called **Metre**. (See also **Duple Time, Triple Time, Quadruple Time, Quintuple Time, Simple Time, Compound Time**)

Time Signature
The pair of figures, one above the other, indicating the time of a piece of music. It is placed at the beginning and at any point where the time changes. The lower figure indicates a note value—e.g., 4 for a crotchet (quarter note)—and the upper figure indicates the number of such units per bar: thus 3/4 means three crotchets in a bar. (See also **Time**)

Toccata
A rapid keyboard piece, exploiting finger 'touch' and dexterity as the name suggests, usually for a single performer. An alternative meaning is a freely composed piece including not only display sections but also contrasting music which is not necessarily fast. This latter type of toccata belongs really to baroque times—e.g., Bach's organ toccatas—but Busoni's rather unwieldy piano Toccata (1921) is of this type. The piano toccatas of Schumann, Ravel, Poulenc etc, are, however, in the **Perpetuum mobile** style.

Tonadilla
A short Spanish comic opera of the 18th and 19th centuries, a successor of the **Zarzuela** and more or less the equivalent of the early Italian **Opera Buffa**. *Tonadillas* sometimes had a small cast, perhaps only three or four characters, and were topical in style, tuneful and dancelike. They gave way around 1850 to new kinds of *zarzuela*.

Tonality
The key system: the kind of musical law that gives precedence, both melodically and harmonically, to a chosen tonic or keynote. Whether this is a natural fact arising from acoustics, or as some would assert purely a matter of convention, is debatable—though most musicians consider the former view to be proven. Certainly evidence taken from all periods and cultures suggests that tonality is indeed natural. This does not, however, mean that extensions of the classical diatonic system need be unfruitful: indeed the diatonic system, though a product of tonality, does not by any means cover the whole field of tonal music, and if this fact were more fully understood there would be fewer sterile arguments as to the merits or otherwise of various compositional methods. (See also **Key, Key Relationship**)

Tone
A word with several possible meanings. (1) In American usage, a sound of definite pitch and duration—i.e., what the British call a 'note'. Also (2), the interval of a major second—i.e., twice a semitone. Also (3), a section of plainchant (Gregorian tone). Finally (4), the **Resultant Tone** and other such tones of acoustical theory.

Tone Cluster
A chord, commonly of adjacent notes on a keyboard (and thus dissonant) produced by the use of the fist, forearm or special implement. A term invented by Henry Cowell (1897–1965), who used the technique, as did Ives.

Tone Poem
Same as **Symphonic Poem**.

Tone-row
Arrangement of tones (notes) as in **Twelve-note Music** or other serial technique.

Tonguing
In wind instrument technique, the use of the tongue for slow or rapid articula-

tion—e.g., by forming t, t–k, and t–k–t consonantal groups, and also for **Fluttertonguing**.

Tonic Accent
See **Accent**.

Tonic Sol-fa
An English method of **Solmisation** for

Miss Glover of Norwich with her tonic sol-fa system, around 1835. It was her method that John Curwen perfected and publicised.

singing, perfected if not invented by John Curwen in the 1840s. The notes of the major scale are called *do, re, mi, fa, sol* (or *soh*), *la, ti* and the octave *do*, abbreviated in score to d, r, m, f, s, l, d̄ or d'. The lower octave notation is an underlined d or d,. The minor scale is from *la* upwards. Tonic sol-fa is really only suitable for diatonic music that modulates infrequently. However, flats and sharps can be denoted by changes of vowel—e.g., sharpened fourth *fe* instead of *fa*, flattened third *ma* instead of *mi*. And there are additional signs indicating metre and note values.

Touch

The skill in operating the key of a piano (and perhaps some other instruments): not the same as neatness or dexterity, but implying some delicate control over timbre and dynamics obtained by the manner in which the keys are depressed. How far piano timbre (tone quality) is affected by touch is debatable. Certainly the kind of praise bestowed on a player's 'touch' is often misplaced—it may be the dynamic balance between tune and accompaniment which is musicianly, or the phrasing, or the pedalling, or more likely all of these in combination.

Tranquillo

Calm.

Transcription

An arrangement of a piece of music —e.g., for another instrument or instruments, perhaps with some degree of elaboration and extension. (See **Arrangement**)

Transformation of Themes

Modification of a theme or themes so that a change of character, but not of identity, takes place. The *idée fixe* in Berlioz's *Symphonie Fantastique* undergoes such changes according to the point in the 'programme' that has been reached. So do themes in Liszt's music—e.g., the *Faust Symphony*, the symphonic poem *Les Préludes* and the Piano Sonata. Wagner also applies this technique to his operatic **Leitmotive** as have later composers—e.g., Britten in his operas. The technique is commonest in programmatic and literary works, but also occurs elsewhere—e.g., Schubert's 'Wanderer' Fantasy for piano (an early example) and Franck's Symphony as well as the Liszt Sonata mentioned above.

Transition

A linking passage—i.e., a **Bridge Passage**. A rarer meaning implies a brief or abruptly-effected key change.

Transposition

Movement of a passage or complete piece into another key—i.e., a change of written pitch—up or down. This is often helpful for a singer when a song lies uncomfortably for the voice. A transposing instrument is one, such as the clarinet in its various sizes, where the player always reads the same note for the same fingering, while the actual notes sounded are different—e.g., a tone lower for the clarinet in B flat. For convenience both of notation and reading, a piccolo part is written one octave below sounding pitch and a double bass part one octave above sounding pitch.

Treble

The unbroken boy's voice, with a range fairly similar to a soprano's, say two octaves from A below the treble clef to the A above that clef. The timbre, however, is quite different and has its own transient beauty.

Tre corde

Literally, 'three strings'. A cancellation of the **Una corda** marking in piano music—i.e., an instruction to release the soft pedal.

Tremolo

The quick reiteration of a note, on a bowed stringed instrument, performed by rapid to-and-fro (technically, 'up' and 'down') movements of the bow. Or the equally rapid alternation of two notes during one long bow or, less commonly, with separate movements of the bow.

Similar effects are possible, to some extent at least, on other instruments such as the guitar and harp, wind and keyboard. A vocal tremolo implies a **Vibrato** that deviates perhaps excessively in pitch.

Triad

A chord of three notes, formed on a degree of the major or minor scale by adding the third and fifth above it. The major triad (e.g., C, E, G) and minor triad (e.g., D, F, A) both occur in major and minor scales alike. So does the diminished triad (e.g, B, D, F). The augmented triad (e.g., C, E, G sharp) occurs on the third degree of the harmonic minor scale. A triad may be in **Root** position, as those so far listed, or in either of two **Inversions**, placing its two other notes in turn as the bass.

Tricinium

A 16th-century vocal composition in three polyphonic parts—e.g., those of the German composer Michael Praetorius.

Trill

A rapid alternation of a note with the note one scale degree above it, indicated by writing the lower note with the sign *tr* above it. If the scale degree is sharpened or flattened, the sharp or flat sign is added.

Trio

A work for three instruments, commonly in four movements and in sonata form. The combination of violin, cello

One of Haydn's piano (or harpsichord) trios, published by Artaria of Vienna

and piano is the most usual; the string trio of violin, viola and cello is much less commonly met with. Another meaning of the term 'trio' is for the central section of a minuet.

Trio Sonata

A contrapuntal work of the baroque period, commonly for two violins and bass, the latter part involving both a stringed instrument and the harpsichord. As regards form, it was either a *sonata da camera* or a *sonata da chiesa*. (See also **Camera**, **Chiesa**)

Triplet

A group of three notes to be played in the time usually taken by two of the same nominal value.

Triple Time

Three beats in a bar—e.g., simple triple 3/8, 3/4 and 3/2, compound triple 9/8, 9/4.

Tritone

The interval of three tones—i.e., the augmented fourth such as occurs between the fourth and seventh degrees of the diatonic scale—e.g., F–B in C major or minor. The diminished fifth B–F is not usually called a tritone, being acoustically different. At one time this interval was called the **Diabolus in Musica**.

Trope

Early musical addition to the plainchant music of the Christian liturgy, from the 9th century onwards—say a **Sequence** or an extension to the *Kyrie*.

Troppo

Too (much)—e.g., *Presto ma non troppo*, quick, but not too much so.

Troubadours

Poet-musicians of southern France, many of whom were of gentle birth. Their songs, of which some three hundred have been preserved, are commonly on the subject of courtly love. William, Duke of Aquitaine, was a troubadour, as were Bernard de Ven-

tadour and Guiraut Riquier. The language of these songs was the *langue d'oc*.

Trouvères

Poet-musicians of northern France, writing in the *langue d'oïl*. Over a thousand of their songs have survived to the present day. The King of Navarre, Thibaut (1201–53), left over sixty songs, many being settings of love poems.

Tune

Melody or theme. The term is sometimes very loosely used simply to mean a piece of music. (See **Tuning**)

Tuning

Adjustment of an instrument—e.g., a stringed instrument, strings of a piano, pipes of an organ etc.—so that it produces notes of correct intonation.

Turba

Choral passage in oratorio, Passion music etc, in which the chorus represents 'the crowd'.

Turca

A passage or whole piece marked *alla turca*, such as the finale of Mozart's A major Piano Sonata, K.331, is supposed to be 'in Turkish style', at least as it was imperfectly understood in Europe during the 18th and 19th centuries from the playing of bands.

Turn

A melodic ornament around a principal note. Rhythmically it takes various forms.

Tutti

Literally 'all'. Thus, a passage for full orchestra, orchestra without the soloist in a concerto, all the singers in a vocal group etc.

Twelve-note Music

A compositional style of the 20th century devised by Schoenberg (1874–1954). It abandons key (tonality) and instead uses as a basis a chosen order (series, row) consisting of all twelve notes within the

U

octave. It is the *order* of the notes that constitutes their identity: they may be heard melodically or harmonically, but the correct sequence is maintained. Thus notes 6 and 7 may be heard consecutively or simultaneously, but not before note 5. Certain specific variants of the order are however permissible: the inversion, retrograde form and retrograde inversion.

There has been heated controversy over the merits of the twelve-note method, and the works written according to its principles. It first reached the concert hall in the 1920s, and Schoenberg, together with his disciples Berg and Webern, adopted the method wholeheartedly. After World War II it found increasing acceptance among composers, Stravinsky for example adopting at least some of its principles in his later works. The Italian Dallapiccola (b. 1904) and the Greek Skalkottas (1904–49)—pupils of Berg and Schoenberg respectively—used the method extensively. Younger composers born since about 1920 (Nono, Boulez, Stockhausen, Maxwell Davies) have used **Serial** techniques but without the twelve-note strictness. Today, some sixty years after the inception of twelve-note writing, a slow integration of some of these ideas (e.g. the intervallic method) seems to be taking place.

Dodecaphony is another name for twelve-note music.

Una corda
An instruction to use the soft pedal on the piano. The use of the phrase *una corda*, 'one string', is explained by the action of this pedal, which on a grand piano moves the keyboard and hammers to the right so that the hammers only strike one (or two) strings instead of the usual three. The direction *tre corde* cancels the *una corda* marking.

Unessential Note
A melodic dissonance such as an **Appoggiatura**, **Passing Note**, as opposed to an 'essential note' which is harmonically part of a chord.

Unison
At the same pitch—i.e., voices or instruments performing the same notes. Rhythmic unison is also possible: this is implied by words such as homophony and homorhythm.

Upper Partials
Same as **Harmonics**.

Up Beat
The Weak beat preceding a bar line; also the conductor's baton (or arm) action indicating such a beat, for example, as a preliminary signal to commence on the down beat immediately following.

Utility Music
Same as **Gebrauchsmusik**.

V

Valves

The piston or rotary mechanism fitted to some brass instruments—e.g., horns, trumpets and tubas, in order to alter their playing length and thus their pitch. Three valves, used singly and in combination, allow six semitones to be reached below a natural (open) note with little change of lip position. A fourth 'compensation valve' may correct faults in intonation occurring when the ordinary valves are used in combination.

Variation

A reworking of material already stated. Variation form originated in the 16th century. It consists of a theme followed by a series of sections, of more or less the same length, each of which presents the theme in a different way. The alterations in the theme may be melodic (embellishments), harmonic (changing from major to minor), rhythmic (a march might become a waltz) and so on. Naturally any or all of these and other changes may be combined. However, classical variations, such as Beethoven's Thirty-two Variations in C minor for piano (1806) are commonly straightforward and even strict. In romantic times the treatment of variation form became markedly freer. Brahms's 'St Antoni' Variations (1873) and Elgar's 'Enigma' Variations (1899), both for orchestra, and Britten's Variations on a Theme of Frank Bridge (1937) for string orchestra represents this later and richer kind of variation form. As the variations proceed there is usually some feeling of progress towards an eventual resolution in a final variation which may be especially substantial—e.g., a fugal treatment of the theme—or alternatively may have an envoi-like quality, as an epilogue.

Vaudeville

Originally, in the 17th century, a Parisian street song or ballad: the name comes from Vau de Vire, a valley in France where the song composer Basselin was born. Later, a theatrical entertainment including songs. To all but scholars, the word nowadays just means a variety show without any formal artistic pretensions.

Veloce

Rapid.

Verbunkos
A Hungarian soldiers' dance, danced in uniform and designed for use in recruiting campaigns from about 1780–1850. It has two sections, one slow (*lassu* or *lassan*) and one fast (*friss*, or *friszka, friska*).

Verismo
Realism, as found in certain operas including Bizet's *Carmen*, Leoncavallo's *Pagliacci*, Puccini's *La Bohème* and Berg's *Wozzeck* and *Lulu*, perhaps in increasing degree so that the most recent of these works (those by Berg) have an especial starkness that might not have been acceptable to a 19th-century audience. All these works have topical themes and deal with 'ordinary people' in un-heroic situations; they are thus very different from older operas whose characters were gods, heroes etc. There is a direct correspondence with the realistic and naturalistic schools in literature exemplified by Flaubert and Zola. An alternative name is 'naturalism'.

Verse
A stanza of poetry. Or a numbered passage in a Biblical text etc., as in 'chapter and verse'. It can also mean a single metrical line of poetry, but this use of the word is now rare. The word is sometimes used simply to mean 'poetry'.

Vibrato
A slight variation of pitch and perhaps dynamics, applied to a note by a singer or instrumentalist—e.g., violinist, flautist, oboist—in order to make the tone quality more expressive.

Villanella
Italian vocal form of the 16th century, originally from Naples, like a **Madrigal** but more chordal and generally simpler, even rustic in character.

Virtuoso
A performer of exceptional technical ability, whether vocal or instrumental. Hence, a 'virtuoso performance', or a 'virtuoso piece', the latter being a display piece. The term has at times been used somewhat depreciatingly, the implication being that the dazzling technician was not very much more than a musical athlete capable of playing a piece faster than others. But this no longer seems to be so, as is proper; for technical mastery is surely an asset, however fine the artistic judgement of the performer possessing it. Indeed his facility allows the instrument

(Left) Helga Pilarczyk in the title role of Berg's Lulu, *verismo opera in a German production*

Vivace

to seem like a natural extension of his mind, so that no obstacle exists between musical intention and instrumental or vocal realisation.

Vivace
Lively.

Vivo
Same as **Vivace**, lively.

Vocalise
A vocal piece without words—e.g., those by Ravel and Rachmaninov. This is a French word; the English verb 'to vocalise' means to sing in this way. Vocalisation exercises are extensively used in the training of solo singers.

Voice
Obviously, the human voice. The term is also used of a single part in polyphonic writing, whether vocal or instrumental. The 'voicing' of organ pipes is their adjustment of pitch and tone.

Voluntary
An organ piece played before, during or after a service, usually in the Anglican Church. Formerly the term had wider application—e.g., Jeremiah Clarke's so-called *Trumpet Voluntary* which was arranged for orchestra by Sir Henry Wood from a harpsichord piece.

W

Wait
An English town official of the 'watch'. In late renaissance times the waits frequently also formed uniformed bands of musicians, playing for ceremonies and

also singing—e.g., carols at Christmas. Nowadays the waits are amateur carol singers calling at private houses during the Christmas season and collecting money for themselves or for good causes.

Waltz

One of the most famous of all dances, in triple time, probably derived from the Austrian **Ländler** but eventually becoming much more urban and sophisticated. It was immensely popular in Europe dur-

ing the 19th century and is indissolubly associated with the Strauss family of Vienna, especially Johann Strauss the Younger (1825–99) who inherited both musical talent and the direction of a famous orchestra from his father. Other composers of waltzes include Schubert, Chopin, Berlioz (in the *Symphonie Fantastique*), Brahms, Tchaikovsky, Richard

A carol-seller singing to advertise his wares in England, 1869. The artist is Cuthbert Bede.

Strauss and Ravel. The famous 'Diabelli'
Variations for piano by Beethoven were
upon a waltz theme by Diabelli.

(Above) The waltz

Whole Note
Same as a semibreve, written ○

Whole-tone Scale
The six-note scale consisting entirely of tones—e.g., C, D, E, F sharp, G sharp, B flat (or A sharp) and its transposition beginning on C sharp. It is clear that any further transposition simply gives one or other of these again, starting on another note. The absence of tone-semitone differences gives this scale a curiously fluid quality, and like the chromatic scale it does not reveal a clear tonic. It features in some of Debussy's music—e.g., the piano prelude *Voiles*—but it is mistaken to assume that he used it consistently or that he is the only composer to have employed it.

Wolf
A note of uneven, or even poor tone quality occurring on stringed instruments of the violin family, perhaps especially the cello. It cannot be wholly cured, being due to vibrations of the belly (front) which are an inevitable outcome of the design.

Word Painting
A detailed parallelism in vocal music, such as is found in the word-setting of the English madrigalists. If the text refers to ascent or descent, for example, the music does likewise; if a goddess is left 'all alone' it is a solo voice that tells us. Bach also uses the technique in his cantatas and Passion music—for example the crowing of the cock at Peter's betrayal, faithfully echoed in the Evangelist's onomatopoeic phrase. But it is probably true that the majority of late renaissance and baroque composers use the technique from time to time, if not habitually.

Working-out
Same as **Development**.

Xácara
Same as **Jácara**.

Y Z

Yodelling

A Swiss and Tyrolean unaccompanied outdoor singing style for the male voice, without words, using the **Falsetto** as well as the usual range. The effect is both cheerful and powerful and the tunes sung have a pleasant rustic quality. Evidently Pygmies in Africa use a similar singing style.

Zapateado

A Spanish solo dance, in triple time, with the rhythm strongly marked by stamping on the ground: a kind of clog-dance.

Zarzuela

Spanish type of opera, taking its name from the Zarzuela Palace near Madrid. There is spoken dialogue as well as music. The *zarzuela* emerged in the 17th century, at the time of the dramatist Calderón: it was a form to which he himself contributed—e.g., his *Celos aun del aire matan* (1662), with music by Juan Hidalgo. The much lighter **Tonadilla** succeeded the original *zarzuela*, however, in the 18th century and it was not until the middle of the 19th century that a wider operatic style again emerged. The subjects of the new *zarzuelas* were not necessarily light and indeed the three-act *zarzuela grande* is 'grand opera'—e.g., Tomas Bretón y Hernández's *La Dolores* (1895). On the other hand the *género chico* of *zarzuela* (or *zarzuelita*) was a comic piece in a single act—e.g., Bretón's *La Verbena de la Paloma* (1894). Later operatic composers have included Pedrell, Falla, Granados, Pahissa, Usandizaga and Guridí.

Znamenny Chant

The early Christian chant of the Russian Orthodox Church from the 11th century onwards to the 17th century, deriving its name from the word *znak*, sign, as applied to the **Neumes** in which this chant was first notated, also called *znamiona*. Arguably it reached its highest achievements with the Novgorod School around the 16th century. In the 17th century polyphonic singing was officially adopted by the Russian Church. A collection of *Znamenny* chants was published in stave notation in 1772, by the order of the Holy Synod.

ACKNOWLEDGMENTS

The illustrations are reproduced by kind permission of the following: Greater London Council 6; Universal Edition (London) Ltd London 8; Trustees of the British Museum 11; Royal College of Music 14; Mary Evans Picture Library 15, 106, 154–5, 156; Anthony Crickmay 16–17; Victoria & Albert Museum 18 (top); Novosti Press Agency 18 (bottom); Museo Nazionale, Palermo 20; Stadtmuseums, Munich 21; Bildarchiv d. Österreichische, Vienna 22, 126–7; Valerie Wilmer 23; Raymond Mander and Joe Mitchenson Theatre Collection 28, 112, 144; William L. Clements Library, University of Michigan 28–9; British Library 30, 50, 84, 149; Reproduced by gracious permission of Her Majesty the Queen 31, 81; Furstlicke Oettigen-Wallerstein'sche Bibliothek und Kunstsammlungen, Schloss Harburg 32–3; New York Public Library 33, 55; Museum für Kunst und Gewerbe, Hamburg 36; Annetta Hoffnung and Dobson Books Ltd, London 39; Archiv für Kunst und Geschichte, Berlin 40–1; Internationale Stiftung Mozarteum, Salzburg 45; Hamlyn Group Picture Library 46, 68, 74; Vytas Valaitis/Camera Press Ltd, London 47; A. Buttmann, Hamburg 48; A.C.L. Brussels 53; Popperfoto Ltd, London 59; Stadtbibliothek, Vienna 62; Biblioteca Ambrosiana, Milan 64; Staatliche Museen Preussischer Kulturbesitz, Berlin 66; William Ransom Hogan Jazz Archive, Tulane University, New Orleans 72; Max Jones Files 73; Eric Auerbach 76; National Portrait Gallery 82; Bibliothèque Nationale, Paris 87, 96, 98–9; Staatliche Kunstsammlungen, Dresden 92; John R. Freeman & Co./Prints and Drawing department of the British Museum 100–1; Helga Wallmüller 102–3 (bottom); Knut H. Evensen 102 (top); Department of Archaeology, Government of Maharashtra, Bombay 116–17; J & W Chester/Wilhelm Hansen London Ltd 118–19; Adrian Boot 120 (bottom); Mansell Collection 122, 124; Biblioteca Nacional, Madrid 131; Houston Rogers 136; Duncan Schiedt 139; Bayerische Staatsgemäldesammlungen, Munich 141; Newberry Library, Chicago 142–3; Günter Englert 152–3.